Formerly
New Directions for
Mental Health Services

Gil G. Noam
Editor-in-Chief

YO-EGZ-884

NEW DIRECTIONS FOR YOUTH DEVELOPMENT

Theory
Practice
Research

summer | 2003

Youth Facing Threat and Terror

Supporting Preparedness and Resilience

Robert D. Macy
Susanna Barry
Gil G. Noam

issue
editors

JOSSEY-BASS
A Wiley Imprint
www.josseybass.com

Youth Facing Threat and Terror:
Supporting Preparedness and Resilience
Robert D. Macy, Susanna Barry, Gil G. Noam (eds.)
New Directions for Youth Development, No. 98, Summer 2003
Gil G. Noam, Editor-in-Chief

Microfilm copies of issues and articles are available in 16mm and 35mm, as well as microfiche in 105mm, through University Microfilms Inc., 300 North Zeeb Road, Ann Arbor, Michigan 48106-1346.

ISSN 1533-8916 (print)   ISSN 1537-5781 (online)

New Directions for Youth Development is part of The Jossey-Bass Psychology Series and is published quarterly by Wiley Subscription Services, Inc., A Wiley company, at Jossey-Bass, 989 Market Street, San Francisco, California 94103-1741. Postmaster: Send address changes to New Directions for Youth Development, Jossey-Bass, 989 Market Street, San Francisco, California 94103-1741.

Subscriptions cost $75.00 for individuals and $149.00 for institutions, agencies, and libraries. Prices subject to change. Refer to the order form at the back of this issue.

Editorial correspondence should be sent to the Editor-in-Chief, Dr. Gil G. Noam, Harvard Graduate School of Education, Larsen Hall 601, Appian Way, Cambridge, MA 02138 or McLean Hospital, 115 Mill Street, Belmont, MA 02478.

Cover photograph by Getty Images.

www.josseybass.com

Contents

Issue Editors' Notes

THREAT, TERROR, AND TRAUMA have, unfortunately, become watch-words of the early twenty-first century. This stems not only from the events of September 11, 2001, or from international armed conflict but from the corrosive stress of poverty and violence in many young people's lives. When traumatic threats have become commonplace in urban life and when war and terror have also become part of the day-to-day experience, we must explore how to prepare, as parents, teachers, clinicians, or youth workers. What do we need to know in order to best support children and youth? Should different types of threats and exposures to violence be addressed differently? Should preparations and interventions differ depending on the age of the child?

This issue of NDYD will examine the effects of threat, stress, and traumatic events, including acts of terror, on children and youth. It is intended to help those who care for children—clinicians, youth and community workers, teachers and parents—to support resolution and recovery. What we know about individual trauma and trauma treatment has been considerably advanced in the past decade, and what we have learned is significant. We must also deepen our understanding of everyday traumas and threats as well as our approaches to collective threats such as natural disasters and terror. Indeed, this volume addresses not only the individual repercussions of threat but also a collective approach to threat. This is essential information for youth service professionals, who are often charged with the care of groups of children when a threatening incident occurs, as were the day-care providers and teachers around the World Trade Center on September 11.

NEW DIRECTIONS FOR YOUTH DEVELOPMENT, NO. 98, SUMMER 2003 © WILEY PERIODICALS, INC.

This volume is only one step in the process of enhancing our shared knowledge. Rather than present a broad-based survey of the field, the editors have chosen to focus mainly on one approach, developed by the Center for Trauma Psychology and the Trauma Center-Boston. This center's work supports youth through community-wide response networks and with prevention and intervention tools, including a systematic, activity-based *stress inoculation* that can be conducted in school and after-school settings to help young people cope with what they may face in the future. From the center's experience, this volume illustrates important ways to prevent traumatic situations from having lifelong, negative impacts. These methods involve providing immediate intervention and fostering safety as soon as a threatening incident has occurred. This approach is also helping to prepare children for future threats through a stress inoculation curriculum that is designed to enhance feelings of safety rather than raise anxiety.

Chapter One presents an overview of threat and trauma that examines the pathways between exposure to life-threat, subsequent prolonged fear responses, and the development of maladaptive behaviors in the service of survival (including concomitant behavioral health and learning disorders). Chapters Two and Three present a conceptual and practice framework for addressing collective threats. The development of trauma response networks is outlined in detail in Chapter Two. This discussion also examines youth intervention protocols designed to identify internal and external resources for youth exposed to difficult and traumatic circumstances and to augment normal recovery, over a normal period of time, using the child's adaptational responses to create safety experiences. These protocols also continually screen for those youth who will require more intensive support including clinical and medical supports.

Chapter Three introduces a state-of-the-art stress inoculation curriculum and explores how it has been developed and used, showing us that prevention is possible and useful and that we need not limit ourselves to responding and reacting to existing threats. Chapter Four presents the findings on violence and threat when youth themselves engage in threatening behavior, as has happened with the rise of right-wing youth in Germany.

The remaining chapters are "think pieces" that consider the effects on children of various large-scale threats. Chapter Five describes the former Yugoslavia's response to the need for trauma specialists after traumatic war crimes and parental separation affected masses of children. This response has included the establishment of a whole new curriculum to address the needs of the people. Chapter Six asks, How has the ongoing threat of war affected Iraqi children? High levels of fear among Iraqi children are evident, and the magnitude of this threat, as well as the duration of the distress, may have unforeseeable, long-term effects. Chapter Seven provides a look at how our most vulnerable children fared before and after the events of September 11—and at how unprepared we were to protect them. Looking forward, we must improve our ability to support children in the face of both everyday threats and major traumatic events.

What all these chapters have in common is a significant commitment to examining how particular approaches to working with children may in fact augment the restoration of children's joy and ultimately their hope. The topics raised throughout these chapters are vitally important, and this is not the only issue of NDYD that will be devoted to them. We still have a long way to go to ensure that children who face threat and terror will have access to care systems that understand how to help these youth have a chance to end up strong and resilient, not chaotic or enraged.

Early intervention in traumatic and threatening situations is a critical ingredient in fostering the resilience that can grow out of adversity. All of us who have contributed to this volume owe a debt of gratitude to the children we have had the honor of working with and who continue to "supervise" our work. Helping children heal from threat requires all of us, as youth intervention leaders, to stay wholly alert and fully open to a deep personal humility and spiritual courage in order to rebuild the safety and the joy children will continue to seek, no matter how great the fears and threats they might face. In this rebuilding we must help youth see the choices they have to bring about their own healing in order that they may regain some control over their lives.

Robert D. Macy
Susanna Barry
Gil G. Noam
Issue Editors

Acknowledgements

The following individuals and institutions have played an important role in supporting our efforts toward developing tools for mental health prevention and intervention services for youth, and we wish to thank them for their invaluable commitment.

On behalf of the Boston Center for Trauma Psychology

Karl Peterson, James Foley, Michael Kineavy, Dicki Johnson Macy, Clifford Robinson, Mary Lou Sudders, Thomas Menino, Linda Sahovey, Roger Solomon, Pam Chamorro, Madelyn Gould, Nesrin Sahin, Tuncay Ergene, Rune Stuvland, Per Ole Tomassen, Ibrahim Masri, Steven Gross, Pamela Brighton, Robert DeMartino, Malcolm Gordon, Neil Boothby, Atle Dyregrov, Bessel van der Kolk, Alex Cook, Ros Moore, Joseph Spinazzola, Kevin Becker, Anthony Raynes, Marcia Hoch, Roy Ettlinger, Robert Anda, Joan Mikula, William Harris, Deborah Rozelle, Massachusets Department of Mental Health-Metro Boston, Massachusetts Counseling Network, Substance Abuse & Mental Health Services Administration, Federal Emergency Management Agency, United States Agency for International Development, Save the Children, UNICEF

On behalf of the Program in Afterschool Education and Research and the RALLY prevention programs

Barbara and Bill Boger, Robert Kargman, Richard & Ronay Menschel, Edward & Ellen Roche Relief Fund, John W. Alden Trust, L.G. Balfour Foundation, Fleet Bank, Lowenstein Foundation,

Mabel A. Horne Trust, Nellie Mae Education Foundation, Partners Community Benefits Program, The After-School Corporation, The Robert Bowne Foundation, The Ittleson Foundation Inc., The William F. and Juliana W. Thompson Charitable Fund, The Peter and Elizabeth C. Tower Foundation, Tufts Health Plan, Blue Cross Blue Shield of Massachusetts Foundation, United Way Foundation, Boston Mayor's 2:00-to-6:00 After-School Initiative, Hyde Square Task Force, Mary E. Curley Middle School, William H. Taft Middle School, Harvard After-School Initiative, Harvard University Office of the President, Federal Gear Up–U.S. Department of Education, Federal Emergency Management Agency (FEMA) (with Boston DMH & Arbour Health Systems Foundation), Boston Community Learning Centers/Cambridge 21st Century Grant, Federal Work-Study Program

Executive Summary

1. Threat and trauma: An overview

Robert D. Macy, Susanna Barry, Gil G. Noam

This overview examines the prevalence of threat and trauma in the lives of children and youth. The psychobiology of stress, including adaptation to stress and posttraumatic stress disorder (PTSD) are addressed. Common responses after exposure to threat include reexperiencing the event and intrusive thoughts and images, hyperarousal, avoidance and numbing, a sense of a foreshortened future, and shattered assumptions about control and safety. This range of adaptations to stress informs the design of trauma interventions.

2. Community-based trauma response for youth

Robert D. Macy

In the late 1980s and early 1990s in Boston, youth violence, including suicides and drug overdoses, grew at an alarming rate. Macy's Center for Trauma Psychology in affiliation with the Trauma Center-Boston developed trauma response networks that included parents and community leaders, health and mental health clinicians, law enforcement officers, members of the faith community, and many others who could offer support to those youth who had lost their friends and classmates to violence. This community intervention was led by a "golden rule" of youth trauma response: those who

NEW DIRECTIONS FOR YOUTH DEVELOPMENT, NO. 98, SUMMER 2003 © WILEY PERIODICALS, INC.

most feel the impact of trauma or threat event must be afforded an ongoing opportunity to play a central role in the resolution of and recovery from the trauma and its aftermath. The trauma response networks are now part of Boston's infrastructure for supporting youth through a wide variety of threatening events.

---

3. Healing in familiar settings: Support for children and youth in the classroom and community

Robert D. Macy, Dicki Johnson Macy, Steven I. Gross, Pamela Brighton

The development of a state-of-the-art classroom-based intervention for trauma was founded in work done by Macy's Center for Trauma Psychology in Turkey following the devastating earthquakes of 1999. This psychosocial intervention emphasized a specific theme each week, designed to address the needs of children who had experienced severe threat. These themes included "information, safety and stabilization," "awareness, control and self-esteem," "thoughts and reactions during the earthquake," "thoughts and reactions during and after the earthquake," "resource identification and coping skills," and "resource installation and future safety planning." These themes were related to each other in such a way as to provide the children with an opportunity to slowly build safe places in which they could then express the story of their earthquake experiences while identifying present and future resources and coping strategies in a group environment. This intervention has strong implications for both supporting children in the wake of threat and providing them with a stress inoculation curriculum before threatening events occur.

---

4. A culture of threat: Right-wing extremism and negative identity formation in German youth

Wolfgang Edelstein

This chapter explores the fate of a cohort exposed to the sudden breakdown of socialism in Eastern Germany. The breakdown suddenly eliminated social structures, value systems, organizational support patterns, modes of living, and future perspectives of the younger generation. It occurred in conjunction with a widespread humiliation of the parent generation as carriers of past value patterns and social structures, a humiliation vicariously resented by the young. The discussion of the basic model for the emergence of the current right-wing youth culture in Eastern Germany addresses the interactions among long-term historical processes, individual development, and cohort-specific social and situational factors. The historical processes involve the rise of anomie and the corrosion of traditions, institutions, and "habits of the heart." The author discusses how vulnerabilities can be traced to flaws in identity formation and to family processes and how the humiliation, alienation, and deprivation to which adolescents react are linked to local conditions or situational contexts.

5. Capacity building in trauma therapy and trauma research in Bosnia-Herzegovina

Gisela Röper, Maria Gavranidou

When Bosnia-Herzegovina was thrown into war in the summer of 1991, one and a half million people lost their homes and were in flight. About one million people were in camps where systemic raping of women with the goal of impregnating them with the enemy's offspring was introduced as an element of warfare. It was clear from the beginning that the extent of trauma would be enormous and evident for generations to come. In this chapter the authors summarize the former Yugoslavia's response to the population's need for trauma specialists, including the establishment of a new curriculum to address the needs of the people. They also present a summary of trauma-related research projects, including work on the effects of parental separation, the reintegration of returnee children, and the longitudinal effects of coping with trauma. Finally, future directions for research are discussed.

6. *Threat in the life of Iraqi children*
Atle Dyregrov, Magne Raundalen

How has the threat of war affected Iraqi children? This chapter presents research conducted in January 2003 by members of the International Study Team. Results of in-depth interviews indicated high levels of fear among Iraqi children and little communication from adults about the emotional aspects of the threat of war. Although children expressed a sense of hope and optimism for the future, in the end their words displayed a depressive and resigned quality. Questionnaire data showed a high level of intrusive thinking about the threat. Given the magnitude of the possible exposure to and duration of distress evidenced by Iraqi children, there is strong reason to expect that this, in combination with unforeseeable consequences of malnutrition and reduced school attendance, may dramatically reduce the learning potential of youth, especially among the poor. The mental resources of Iraqi parents have been depleted over a long period of time, and in combination with other negative health effects this may have a catastrophic effect on their children's mental health.

7. *Time frames*
William W. Harris

The images of September 11, 2001, are forever ingrained in each of us and in our children. How will we move ahead to prepare for the needs of the future? In this chapter the author considers the needs of U.S. children before, during, and after 9/11. Prior to 9/11, the federal government usually provided programs for children and families in bits and pieces rather than taking the full ecological context into account. The response to the events of 9/11 was evidence of a lack of preparation. The final section of this chapter looks to the future, addressing concerns and offering recommendations about the steps we can take to develop a greater local and national capacity to meet the needs of children and families before, during, and after violent attacks.

Common responses after exposure to threat include reexperiencing the event, intrusive thoughts and images, hyperarousal, avoidance and numbing, a sense of a foreshortened future, and shattered assumptions about control and safety.

1

Threat and trauma: An overview

Robert D. Macy, Susanna Barry, Gil G. Noam

FOR THOSE OF US who work with at-risk youth, it is crucially important to understand that many of the most destructive youth health-risk behaviors are correlated with a childhood history of stressful and threatening experiences. In a seminal 1998 study jointly conducted by Kaiser Permanente's Department of Preventive Medicine in San Diego and the Centers for Disease Control and Prevention (CDC) in Atlanta, results showed that a majority of youth health-risk behaviors leading to teen pregnancy and teen paternity, sexually transmitted diseases, substance abuse, violence, suicide, and homicide were highly correlated with child maltreatment or adverse childhood experiences.[1] For the children and youth who have sustained traumatic stress exposures, these health-risk behaviors may be seen, paradoxically, as attempts at self-protection or self-care, in the service of survival.[2] Some of the general principals of the psychobiology of trauma underscore that many of these attempts at self-protection are in fact normal responses to significantly threatening situations.[3]

NEW DIRECTIONS FOR YOUTH DEVELOPMENT, NO. 98, SUMMER 2003 © WILEY PERIODICALS, INC.

The psychobiology of trauma in youth: Adaptation to stress and posttraumatic stress disorder

Animal and human responses exhibited secondary to threat exposure have been examined for centuries. Hans Selye, a pioneer in the field of modern stress research,[4] defines stress as "the non-specific response of the body to any demands made upon it." Each demand or challenge to the body, each *stressor*, will cause a discrete physiological response. For example, if the body is hot it will perspire, and if cold it will shiver. Increased physical activity will cause alterations in heart rate, blood pressure, and temperature. Selye proposed that whatever the specific physiological response to the stressor might be, there is also activated a nonspecific response that is independent of the stressor.[5] For example, if a spouse is told that his or her partner has died in a car accident, that spouse will suffer a terrible shock and intense psychological distress. If some time later the partner walks into the room alive and well, the spouse will experience extreme relief and joy. The specific results of the stressor are opposite, but the nonspecific effect on the body will be quite similar. The accumulation of stress secondary to exposure to stressors, whether good or bad, if intense enough will ultimately cause physical disorders.

In order to understand the design and development of youth interventions that can reduce health-risk behaviors after life-threatening exposures, it is important to spend a moment examining the differences between normal adaptation to threat, or the *stress response*, and the "breakdown in adaptation to stress."[6] Animals and humans are biologically primed to seek survival data. For example, if a number of people are exposed to the sound of a very loud explosion, their physiological systems will respond in a predictable manner, prior to any planned, cognitive-oriented reaction, in the service of survival. This physiological response to the sound of the explosion, primarily driven by the autonomic nervous system, will begin with a physical startle response (acoustic startle) that elongates the entire body, allowing for continuous scanning of the environment for survival data, followed quickly by a physical withdrawal or shrinking, allowing the body to reduce its target size or exposure, all the while continuing to scan the environment for survival data. These survival data are not only threat data but also safety data, such as determining not only where the explosion is coming from but where the safest retreat or escape route is.

The range of adaptations to perceived physical or psychological aggression and threat is complex, and by necessity the stress response activates both physiological and psychological systems to operate outside regular homeostatic functioning. Progressive modification of the initial response or the seeking of and acting upon survival data, in the service of eliminating the threat while maintaining attachment to safety, involves behavioral transitions over time, augmented by both internal and external resources, and usually brings about adaptive resolutions to the threat or perceived threat, which then allow the system to return to homeostasis.

In some small percentage of individuals the progressive modification of the initial response is delayed, interrupted and halted, or sustained in such a manner as to disallow the system from returning to homeostatic functioning, which in turn may increase the risk of further exposure to the threat. A breakdown in the adaptation to stress occurs whereby the system fixates on threat-related survival data, then critical recognition of and attachment to safety-related survival data diminishes over time. Such a breakdown in the adaptation to stress may have disastrous consequences, including neurobiological alterations that sustain maladaptive responses to everyday challenges. This breakdown in the adaptational response to stress may be considered the initiation of the *process* of posttraumatic stress disorder (PTSD).

In other words, in some small percentage of survivors, the adaptational response to stress and threat can become maladaptive, leading these individuals to risk-taking or self-destructive behaviors (such as substance abuse; unprotected, indiscriminate sex; or truancy), all in an attempt to regain control over their lives. This process, in the absence of intervention, can become a pathological response and, as reviewed in the literature, is *not the norm for some 80 to 90 percent of individuals who are exposed to a traumatic event.*[7] Normally an initial stress response that causes significant impairment in functioning may be diagnosed as *acute stress disorder* (ASD), but if symptoms from the acute stress disorder persist for more than thirty days, a diagnosis of PTSD is to be considered.

As we consider youth exposed to life-threat we must keep in mind, of course, that they are in development and the impact of the exposure will be developmentally dependent. We must also overlay on their developmental trajectory the adaptational response to stress just described. So when we consider how threat and terror may affect a child, it will be key to view her response and develop our intervention pathways along the blended continuum of her psychological development and her adaptational development to the stressor. When children are exposed to overwhelming threat or terrifying events, their bodies react in expectable ways. When children and youth perceive that they are in life-threatening danger, *whether the danger is real or imagined,*[8] their nervous systems respond in accordance with the perceived level of threat, in the service of survival, in order to *adapt to the challenges* presented by the threat exposure.

The interplay between perception and stress response in the face of threat is a fundamental concept that will be examined repeatedly in this issue. What are experienced by youth, in their bodies, as significant challenges from the outside—as threats or stressors—will vary from child to child depending on biological differences in temperament or *vagal tone,*[9] on the age of the child, on his preexposure access to resources, and on his postexposure access to appropriate supports. Thus interventions designed either to prevent the onset of pathological adaptation to threat or to reduce the negative impacts of traumatic stress reactions after threat exposure must assess for these variances in affected youth and provide for a choice of recovery paradigms that support the validity of the child's perception of his threat experience while taking into account his stage of psychological development in conjunction with the adaptational stress response phase he is in at the time of the intervention.[10]

Hans Selye's groundbreaking work on human fear and stress responses delineated some of the normal physiological reactions to threat exposures.[11] During the ensuing investigations on the psychobiology of human stress responses some fundamental discoveries have contributed to our understanding of the mechanisms through which the human nervous system either successfully adapts to threat and terror or experiences adaptation that may become pathogenic.[12] During exposure to acute threat, brain neurophysiology "automatically" begins adjusting to the threat environment, in the service of maintaining homeostasis, by engaging multiple parts of the autonomic nervous system involving neurotransmitters that induce *both* arousal *and* calming. The autonomic nervous system regulates (energizes and calms down) each organ of the body, including lungs, heart, blood vessels, stomach, adrenals, kidneys, pancreas, intestines, bladder, bronchi, trachea, larynx, sweat glands, eyes, tear ducts, and external genitalia.

Over the last four decades this elegant and subtle interplay between the sympathetic nervous system (SNS) and the parasympathetic nervous system (PNS) in adapting to novel or overwhelming stressors has, unfortunately, been reduced in our thinking to three reactions: *fight, flight,* or *freeze,* that is, to SNS functions. A fourth reaction and, perhaps especially for youth, a most essential reaction is *appraisal,* or the state of calm awareness and stillness in action, with the ability to discern what is safe and what is dangerous even during the threat exposure. This essential autonomic survival response is managed by the PNS functions. Although the reduction to fight, flight, or freeze may be useful for a general understanding of the human stress response, it over emphasizes the pathogenic components of adaptation to threat and obscures the potential health-producing effects, via the PNS functions, of threat exposure, a process that may be understood as *salutogenesis.* Indeed, normal responses to overwhelming fear and threat are managed by the SNS and will usually include both the fight and the flight response, sometimes occurring at the same time! Less frequently, freezing may occur, especially if the autonomic nervous system is unable to produce an immediate action response that reduces the imminent danger. This freezing is a form of submission, an attempt to appease the aggressor, in the service of survival. This is especially relevant for children and youth, who have less survival practice, less life experience, and less access to resources when confronted with threat and may engage more frequently in the freeze reaction.

As the chapters in this volume demonstrate it is especially important for youth interventionists to consider how to assess and mitigate the negative effects of a freezing or submission response experienced by children and youth during a crisis, as this experience can lead later to significant impairments in self-esteem, self-efficacy, self-soothing, and affect regulation capacities.[13] Ultimately the objective of the psychosocial interventions that will be examined in this issue, particularly the stress inoculation components, is to allow youth to practice active appraisal strategies, in a safe environment, in order to reduce the possibility of their freezing during a real life-threat exposure.

So far, this discussion has outlined the primary responses of the SNS as it manages perceived or real threat and terror scenarios. Before we review what can happen to youth when their adaptive responses to threat and terror are unsuccessful and may therefore produce health-risk behaviors, let's briefly examine the "management techniques" of the PNS. If the SNS is responsible for giving the "green light" to protect survival at whatever cost, the PNS is responsible for giving the "red light" that allows the system to *stop* fighting or fleeing, to rest, to regenerate, to rebuild, to reconstruct meaning out of a meaningless event, to recognize and allow for the experience of safety and secure attachment. What is interesting about the design of the autonomic nervous system is that when threat exposure occurs, *both* the SNS *and* the PNS are activated *at the same time*, again in the service of maintaining homeostasis. So the experience is one of facing *both* the green light *and* the red light together. This dual response, known in neurology lingo as *reciprocal innervation*, is by no means an accident. As we face a life-threat, real or imagined, different neurochemicals are surging into our bloodstream to prepare us for the fight or the flight (SNS) and at the same time to prepare our bodies to conserve precious energy (PNS—our appraisal system) until it is truly needed for the fight or flight and to appraise the level of danger we face *and* the level of resources we have available to adapt to the threat.

Therefore the primary functions of the PNS include

- Modulation of our SNS energies, in the face of life-threat, so that we don't pump more arousal chemicals (the fight or flight energy) into our organs and bloodstream than we actually need to deal with the threat
- Innervating (switching on) our appraisal system so that we can recognize when the danger is over and stop the fight and flight reactions
- Innervating our appraisal system so that once we recognize the danger is over we allow ourselves to reduce threat detection behaviors and begin safety-seeking behaviors or behaviors that seek secure attachments (explained in great detail later)

As this volume hopes to demonstrate, carefully structuring the reduction of threat detection behaviors while guiding and supporting successful safety seeking and ultimately assisting youth with the navigation of seeking secure attachments after their experience of sudden, violent loss, may be one of the most important outcomes any youth intervention can provide. As part of the unfortunate but perhaps medically necessary reductionism referenced earlier, many assessment and intervention paradigms addressing youth exposure to threat, terror and sudden, violent loss focus predominately on the SNS trajectory or the development of pathological adaptation to stressors, to the extent that PTSD and the traumatized child have almost become household words post–September 11, 2001. Although understandable, especially given the events of 9/11 and the ensuing aftermath of terrorist threats, the authors in this volume hope to offer a complementary view and concomitant intervention protocols that focus predominantly on the natural regulatory interactions between the SNS and PNS in youth exposed to threat and terror and that demonstrate methods for augmenting normal recovery in normal children having normal reactions over a normal period of time to abnormal events.

This is not to diminish the importance of identifying youth at risk after threat exposure and carefully assessing and treating these youth if they have become symptomatic due to exposure. Some basic behavioral reactions that begin as normal reactions to an abnormal event may in fact end up supporting maladaptive coping strategies and lead to anxiety disorders such as generalized anxiety disorder, phobias, panic attacks, and as outlined earlier, acute and posttraumatic stress disorders.

Basic categories of responses to threat or traumatic stress reactions that may require more intensive clinical treatment if they do not abate over time (usually within thirty days) include the following.

Reexperiencing the event and intrusive thoughts and images

This reaction is one of the hallmarks of posttraumatic stress. The survivor reexperiences the event, even weeks after the event is over. Behaviors associated with this response include sleep disturbances, nightmares, night terrors, and unbidden intrusive thoughts, memories or detailed disturbing images of the traumatic experience. Among youth these images may be repeatedly expressed in artwork or reenactment play or verbal storytelling.

Hyperarousal

Although hyperarousal serves a primary function in threat detection, when it continues after the danger has subsided, the child's mind and body remain in a constant state of alert. The behaviors associated with this state are hypervigilance, heightened startle response, being easily triggered by stimuli that remind the child of traumatic experiences, irritability, and repetition of behaviors associated with the most subjectively disturbing aspect of the traumatic experience. These behaviors may continue, even when the child is in a safe environment, because the child does not yet perceive that she is safe. Her green light is still active, and her red light has not been activated.

Avoidance and numbing

In this response the child's mind and body are numb, or the child avoids any stimulus that reminds him of the traumatic event(s). Some of the behaviors associated with avoidance and numbing states are avoidance of thoughts, emotions, or places connected with the traumatic experience; social withdrawal; pronounced forgetfulness or "spaceyness"; low mood or depression; an extremely restricted range of emotions; and failure to recognize current threats and risks, often resulting in dangerous, risk-taking behaviors.

Sense of a foreshortened future

The child may sense that her locus of control is no longer internal but rather external, meaning that the child senses that no matter what she does, someone or something else *outside* of her is in control of her life events. Children (and adults) may then begin to perceive their world as having no future, thinking, in effect: "If something terrible happened to me once, it can certainly happen again because I have no control over what happens to me. I am doomed, no matter what."

These kinds of reactions can occur in children who have survived a traumatic experience directly or in those have who witnessed a traumatic event or have heard about or known someone who experienced such an event. It is important to recognize that "vicarious" traumatization or secondary trauma can have the same effect on children as a direct trauma.

Shattered assumptions

Although this list of traumatic stress responses is certainly not exhaustive, they are the primary domains that should be assessed and monitored after a life-threat event. Associated with these four primary domains of posttraumatic stress is the phenomenon of meaning making after a traumatic event, or the experience of shattered assumptions.[14] Basic assumptions that are active and relied upon prior to a traumatic exposure include these:

I am in control. (Child: My parents are in control.)
I am safe. (Child: My parents will keep me safe.)

Bad things happen to other people; bad things can't happen to me.
  (Child: My parents won't let bad things happen to me.)
I am worthy, and life has meaning.

Life-threat, terror, and traumatic experiences will usually affect children's core beliefs regarding their sense of self and the world. Basic assumptions tend to be shattered after exposure to a traumatic event and then may be reconstituted in these forms:

I am not in control, and my adult caregivers are not in control either.
I am not safe, and my adult caregivers were unable to keep me safe.
Bad things can happen to me, and if they happened once they can happen again.
If these kind of bad things can happen to me, I must deserve this; I must have done something wrong; I must not be worthy of safety.

Shattered assumptions can cause significant cognitive disruptions. Basic needs, including the need for safety, self-esteem, control, trust, and intimacy are disrupted, as are other important frames of reference, including the child's self-identity[15]; the child's ability to organize and assess effectively; the child's spiritual beliefs; and the child's view that the world is a safe place. Finally, the child experiences disruptions in how his body functions. The child's memory systems are affected (for example, the child becomes forgetful and cannot focus, concentrate, or memorize, losing the essential ingredients he needs to be a successful learner), and the child experiences problems with sleeping and eating patterns.

Child maltreatment and adverse childhood experiences

Child maltreatment and other adverse childhood experience (ACE) can bring about any of the psychobiological reactions just described. Child maltreatment may be divided into four overlapping areas—neglect, sexual abuse, physical abuse, and the witness-

ing of violence—each of which causes a degradation of psycho-
28social integration and sustained traumatic stress responses and
may lead to permanent disabilities. Felitti and others report the preliminary results of a large-scale study (N = 9,508) examining the relationship of childhood abuse and household dysfunction to many
of the leading causes of death in adults.[16] (This study, illustrated in
Figure 1.1, has become known as the Adverse Childhood Experiences Study.) Categories of adverse childhood experiences (psychological, physical, or sexual abuse; violence against mother; and living
with household members who were substance abusers, had untreated
mental illness, or were suicidal or ever imprisoned) were compared
to measures of adult risk behavior, health status, and disease.

The following list is a brief summary of significant findings from
the 1998 ACE study:

- More than 50 percent of the respondents reported at least one ACE.
- More than 25 percent of the respondents reported at least
  two ACEs.
- Persons who had experienced four or more ACEs had a 4- to 12-
  fold increased health risk for alcoholism, drug abuse, depression,
  and suicide attempt; a 2- to 4-fold increase for smoking, poor
  self-rated health, and sexually transmitted diseases; and a 1.4- to
  1.6-fold increased risk for physical inactivity and severe obesity.
- Adults with four or more ACEs had a 2- to 4-fold increased
  health risk for ischemic heart disease, cancer, chronic pulmonary
  disease, skeletal fractures, and liver disease.

Each year in America over 3 million children are reported as
having been abused and over 1 million cases are substantiated. Each
year in America an estimated 3.3 million[17] to 10 million[18] children
witness violence in the home, ranging from insults to fatal assaults
with knives and guns. In a comparison study of census data from
five cities, domestic violence occurred disproportionately in homes
with children under the age of five. Children in this age group were
more likely than older children to witness multiple acts of domestic violence and substance abuse.[19] In cases of family violence,

Figure 1.1. Adverse childhood experiences

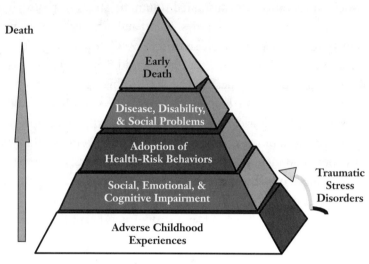

Source: Felitti, V. J., and others (1998). Relationship of childhood abuse to many of the leading causes of death in adults: The adverse experiences (ACE) study. *American Journal of Preventative Medicine, 14*(4), 245–258. Used with permission.

younger children experience more serious injuries than older children do. When children witness violence, *or the threat of violence,* toward a family member or other individuals they care about, the traumatic effect is intensified, and when these acts are witnessed over and over again, the child is at risk for significant developmental delays and severe emotional disturbances.

These children may be the most vulnerable to the long-term debilitating effects of developmental delays and learning disorders and, ultimately, to depression and traumatic stress disorders. The majority of these adverse childhood experiences are not reported or responded to as critical incidents. Therefore no formal psychosocial or psychological trauma intervention is offered. So children and youth exposed to continuous threat and violent experiences tend to adapt in ways that work for them in the moment, in order to relieve immediate fear, anxiety, and the threat of injury or death.

Many of these adaptive responses, although seemingly effective in the moment, build an internal architecture of response to threat that may have serious health and societal consequences, including intense and prolonged substance use and abuse; weapons trafficking; truancy; indiscriminate, promiscuous sex; suicidal thinking; and targeted aggression against siblings and peers.

Violence among youth is an important public health problem. This violence includes peer-to-peer aggression and self-destruction. Between 1985 and 1991, homicide rates among youth fifteen to nineteen years of age increased 154 percent and remain today at historically high levels.[20] Teen suicide has tripled in the last thirty years. Two hundred percent of that increase occurred between 1990 and 1998. The U.S. surgeon general has declared teen suicide a national health emergency.

Youth violence against peers and self should be considered in the context of using maladaptive behaviors in the service of survival. Youth will expose themselves to further threat scenarios in an attempt to gain and maintain the control they did not experience in previously uncontrollable threat situations.

Prior research points to a number of factors that increase the probability of violence during childhood, adolescence, and young adulthood. Some of these factors are the early onset of aggressive behaviors in childhood, social problem-solving skill deficits, exposure to violence, poor parenting practices and poor family functioning, negative peer influences, access to firearms, and neighborhoods characterized by high rates of poverty, transiency, family disruption, and social isolation.[21] Since the terrorist events of 9/11, the concept of psychological trauma and the intervention practices for that trauma have experienced a significant and continuing expansion, perhaps never before seen on such large scale, at least in the United States. Although the need for a broader conceptualization and more refined interventions were imperative prior to the 9/11 attacks, at this point, three months before the second anniversary of that horrific event, we may be witnessing an overinclusive conceptualization of psychological trauma, with the result that parents, teachers, school administrators, policymakers, and even pediatricians now view the majority of adverse experiences encountered by youth as "trauma-tizing. In fact adult caregiving systems are so inundated now by the daily barrage of expert trauma opinions and media trauma editori-als that we have begun to see a negative reaction to the word *trauma*, as if trauma were too much in our world. "Is every kid who goes through a terrible event going to be traumatized . . . going to end up with PTSD?" "I am really getting tired of hearing about youth trauma. . . . [I]t just gives them an excuse not to follow through with good effort and academic work."

Now, this is an unfortunate state of affairs, because most class-room educators and certainly well-trained child trauma clinicians understand that many forms of learning disorders, as well as other debilitating cognitive and behavioral barriers to learning, may indeed have significant trauma exposure as their underlying sub-strate.[22] So although psychological trauma is now in the forefront of our society's consciousness, it may end up being once again min-imized because too many expert professionals are opining, with too little field experience, that large numbers of kids are traumatized and need immediate specialty interventions—interventions that may in many cases pathologize normal and creative adaptive responses to threat and terror.

Effectively addressing these issues requires striking a balance between too much talk of trauma and too little recognition of the serious dysfunction that traumatic stress reactions can cause in youth and their ability to learn, to relate to peers and adults, and to play.[23]

In order to strike such a balance it may be most important to briefly consider the continuum concept of exposure to difficult circumstances or adverse experiences. As described by the Felitti et al. study, perhaps the most adverse experiences, those at the far end of the continuum, are the ones such as neglect, sexual and physical abuse, and continuous witnessing of domestic violence, which threaten the life and psycho-logical integrity of a child. Unfortunately these experiences appear to be more common than most adults in our country may realize.

An important question to address with respect to this continuum concept is the relationship between exposure to trauma and development of a traumatic stress disorder. This question goes to the heart of the previous discussion: when do children's reactions become trauma reactions and when are they adaptive responses? Certain exposures—such as sexual assault and abuse, multiple war experiences, torture, and refugee status—may be considered high risk for initiating and sustaining traumatic stress responses. An important mediating factor is the number and quality of and the accessibility to preincident and postincident resources that youth have available.

In closing, this overview discussion of the psychobiology of trauma and the impact of adverse childhood experiences (ACEs) turns to the prevalence of traumatic exposure and trauma in our own "backyard." Disproportionately large numbers of youth live in poverty in each of our fifty states, as identified by the current Medicaid rolls, and they may be the most vulnerable to the negative sequelae of violence, ACEs, and terrorist attacks. A large epidemiological study, completed by Robert Macy, examining the period prevalence of PTSD among a sample of treatment-seeking Massachusetts Medicaid enrollees aged five years to sixty-four years found that the highest levels of DSM-III-R PTSD were among the five-to-eighteen-year-olds.[24] (See Figure 1.2.) These Medicaid recipients live at or below the poverty level ($10,000 or less annual income) and may therefore be at high risk for continuous exposure to difficult circumstances and lack of resources to assist with coping and recovery.[25] Perhaps most noteworthy, these period prevalence rates are extraordinarily high compared to other published rates, especially considering that the exposures for the Medicaid youth may in many cases be nondiscrete, for example, chronic exposure to degradation, ACEs, and community violence rather than exposures to natural disasters, refugee status, political violence, abuse, or psychiatric illness.

In conclusion, as we seek to understand youth intervention methods that support the recovery from terror and threat, we must first understand the existing levels of continuous threat exposure sustained by our most vulnerable youth and make certain we offer dynamic psychosocial structures that provide some safety at the

Figure 1.2. Period prevalence rates of PTSD as Medicaid study population ages, by age and by gender

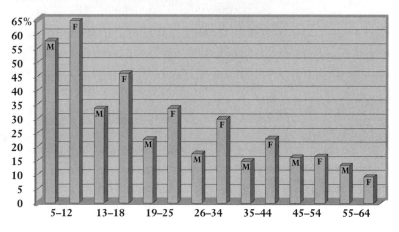

Note: N = 19,775

local level, meaning in the neighborhoods where the trauma and impoverishment are taking place. Given that so many of our communities have faced or will face major threat, the need for effective recovery and prevention protocols is critical.

Notes

1. Felitti, V. J., Anda, R. F., Nordernberg, D., Williamson, D. F., Spitz, A. M., Edwards, V., Koss, M. P., & Marks, J. S. (1998). Relationship of childhood abuse to many of the leading causes of death in adults: The adverse experiences (ACE) study. *American Journal of Preventative Medicine, 14*(4), 245–258.

2. Fischer, K., Ayoub, C., Singh, I. Noam, G., Maraganore, A., & Raya, P. (1997). Psychopathology as adaptive development along distinctive pathways. *Development and Psychopathology, 9,* 749–779.

3. Cicchetti, D., & Lynch, M. (1993). Toward an ecological/transactional model of community violence and child maltreatment: Consequences for children's development. *Psychiatry, 56*(1), 96–118.

4. Selye, H. (1974). *Stress without distress.* New York: New American Library.

5. Selye (1974).

6. Lafontaine, A. (1995). Epidemiology of "stress" and the problems it poses in the medical and social fields: The special case of acute psychic reactions to psychologic trauma. *Bulletin de l'Academie Nationale de Médecine, 179*(3), 449–459.

7. Brunello, N., Davidson, J., Deahl, M., Kessler, R., Mendlewicz, J., Racagni, G., Shalev, A., & Zohar, J. (2001). Posttraumatic stress disorder: Diagnosis and epidemiology, comorbidity and social consequences, biology and treatment. *Neuropsychobiology, 43*(3), 150–162.

8. Sorenson, S. (2002). Preventing traumatic stress: Public health approaches. *Journal of Traumatic Stress, 15*(1), 3–7.

9. Porges, S. W., Doussard-Roosevelt, J. A., Portales, A. L., & Greenspan, S. I. (1996). Infant regulation of the vagal "brake" predicts child behavior problems: A psychobiological model of social behavior. *Developmental Psychobiology, 29*(8), 697–712.

10. Fischer, K. W., & Ayoub, C. (1994). Affective splitting and dissociation in normal and maltreated children: Developmental pathways for self in relationships. In D. Cicchetti & S. L. Toth (Eds.), *Rochester Symposium on Development and Psychopathology: Vol. 5. Disorders and dysfunctions of the self* (pp. 149–222). Rochester, NY: University of Rochester Press.

11. Selye (1974).

12. Yehuda, R., & McFarlane, A. (Eds.). (1997). *Annals of the New York Academy of Sciences: Vol. 821. Psychobiology of posttraumatic stress disorder.* New York: New York Academy of Sciences.

13. Ruscio, A., Weathers, F., King, L., & King, D. (Oct. 2002). Male war-zone veterans' perceived relationships with their children: The importance of emotional numbing. *Journal of Traumatic Stress, 15*(5), 351–357.

14. Janoff-Bulman, R. (1992). *Shattered assumptions: Towards a new psychology of trauma.* New York: Free Press.

15. Cicchetti, D. (1991). Fractures in the crystal: Development of the mental psychopathology and the emergence of self. *Developmental Review, 11,* 271–287.

16. Felitti et al. (1998).

17. Carlson, L. R. (1984, December). No peers in my sphere. *Kansas Nurse, 59*(12), 10–11.

18. Straus, M. A. (1991). Family violence in American families: Incidence rates, causes, and trends. In D. D. Knudsen & J. L. Miller (Eds.), *Abused and battered: Social and legal responses of family violence* (pp. 17–34). Zurich: Aldine de Gruyter.

19. Fantuzzo, J., Boruch, R., Beriama, A., Atkins, M., & Marcus, S. (1997). Domestic violence and children: Prevalence and risk in five major U.S. cities. *Journal of the American Academy of Child and Adolescent Psychiatry, 36*(1), 116–122.

20. Dahlberg, L. L. (1998). Youth violence in the United States: Major trends, risk factors, and prevention approaches. *American Journal of Preventive Medicine, 14*(4), 259–272.

21. Dahlberg (1998).

22. Noam, G. G., Pucci, K., & Foster, E. (1999). Prevention practice in school settings: The Harvard RALLY Project as applied developmental approach to intervention with at-risk youth. In D. Cicchetti & S. Toth (Eds.), *Developmental psychopathology: Developmental approaches to prevention and intervention* (pp. 57–109). Rochester: University of Rochester Press. See also Cicchetti & Lynch (1993).

23. Kane, S., Raya, P., & Ayoub, C. (1997). Pair play therapy with toddlers and preschoolers. In R. Selman, C. Watts, & L. H. Schultz (Eds.), *Fostering*

friendship: Pair therapy for treatment and prevention (pp. 185–206). New York: Aldine de Gruyter.

24. Macy, R. D., & Payne, C. (Submitted for review). *On the epidemiology of posttraumatic stress disorder: Period prevalence rates and acute service utilization rates among Massachusetts Medicaid program enrollees: 1993–1996.*

25. Noam, Pucci, & Foster (1999).

ROBERT D. MACY *is executive director, the Center for Trauma Psychology; codirector, National Center for Child Traumatic Stress Network-Category III; and director, Community Services, the Trauma Center-Boston. In collaboration with codirector Bessel van der Kolk, he is responsible for the Category III design, development, and service delivery management of the national initiative to research and treat child and adolescent posttraumatic stress disorders funded by the Substance Abuse and Mental Health Services Administration. Macy is also the director of psychosocial initiatives at the Trauma Center-Boston and founder of the Community Services Program, which manages the Metro Boston Trauma Response Network for Youth.*

SUSANNA BARRY *is assistant director of the Program in Afterschool Education and Research (PAER) at Harvard.*

GIL G. NOAM *is associate professor of psychiatry/psychology at McLean Hospital and Harvard Medical School and associate professor of education at the Harvard Graduate School of Education. He is the founding director of the PAER.*

The "golden rule" of youth trauma response is that those most affected by the trauma or threat event must be afforded an ongoing opportunity to play a central role in the resolution of and recovery from the trauma and its aftermath.

2

Community-based trauma response for youth

Robert D. Macy

IN BOSTON during the latter part of the 1980s and the first four years of the 1990s, youth violence was growing at an alarming rate, matching the national growth rate in youth homicide and nonfatal penetrating wounds.[1] Although the consistent and creative programming developed by the Boston law enforcement community did an extraordinary job of reducing the rate of youth homicide and youth-on-youth violent attacks in Boston, by the mid-1990s, the psychological aftermath of the high rates of youth homicide left youth survivors at great risk for developing any number of health-risk behaviors, including further targeted aggression behaviors.

This journal issue focuses on the protocols and approach developed by the Center for Trauma Psychology, yet it is important to note one of our collaborations, another Boston-based program designed to work with youth in jeopardy of developing health-risk behaviors. RALLY (Responsive Advocacy for Life and Learning in Youth) is a prevention program built upon evidence-based knowledge about risk, resilience and mentoring. Developed at McLean

NEW DIRECTIONS FOR YOUTH DEVELOPMENT, NO. 98, SUMMER 2003 © ROBERT D. MACY

Hospital, Massachusetts General Hospital, and the Harvard Graduate School of Education, RALLY now serves four Boston schools and is replicated in a number of U.S. cities. It represents a low-cost model for delivering and linking preventative services in school and afterschool settings. Within the RALLY model, a new kind of educator—the prevention practitioner—works closely with teachers and develops strong, supportive relationships with children. These relationships enable the practitioner to better assess children for early signs of psychological and learning difficulties, to make referrals to school-based or community services, and to connect school and afterschool environments to families and community health and mental health providers. The RALLY structure ensures that trauma and threat will be detected and responded to rapidly, since trusting adult-youth relationships are the key to the program's success. For more information about the RALLY program, readers may refer to the Zero Tolerance issue of *NDYD*, or visit www.PAERweb.org. At present, our work at the Trauma Center, under examination in this issue, serves as an in-depth example of the kind of creative programs that are being developed and piloted across the field.

Best practices in youth trauma response and referral protocols were developed between 1990 and 2002 by my multidisciplinary staff and me at the Community Services Program (CSP) of the Trauma Center-Boston. They reflect knowledge acquired from staff members' extensive duty in the field (the streets of Boston), and empirical research findings from diverse disciplines, focusing on both the etiology of traumatic stress disorders and evidence-based effective interventions to reduce acute stress symptoms and some of the adverse affects of child maltreatment (see Chapter One for more information).

These response and recovery protocols are highly structured, phase-oriented, and developmentally specific and include state-of-the-art, risk management, *postvention-recovery* and intervention strategies for youth exposed to threat and terror events. A key concept, or "golden rule," of youth trauma response developed by the CSP during this decade was that those most impacted by the trauma or threat event must be afforded an ongoing opportunity to play a central role in the resolution of and recovery from the trauma and its aftermath. In other words, local "experts," local healers, local teachers, and local mentors must be empowered at their neighborhood level to respond to and guide threatened youth, and fiscal and administrative support for these local responses must be sustained over time until the local infrastructure is stable and self-supporting.

Putting community-based assessment and protocols into action

In 1996, the Metro Boston Department of Mental Health (DMH), decided to put out for competitive bid its block grant funding for its School and Community Support Programs. These monies had been previously used for trauma research, but DMH was now looking to create local infrastructure that could support a community-based trauma response program in Metro Boston. DMH knew what it wanted to accomplish but did not know how to do it. DMH was asking vendors to bid on a contract that required 365/24/7 psychological trauma response for 80,000 youth, and their adult caregiving systems, in their school *and* community environments. And this was to be accomplished for $90,000 per year.

The CSP was awarded this grant; it was to begin service on July 1, 1996. The grant was awarded, in part, because of the CSP's golden rule of youth trauma response: local expertise must be afforded the opportunity to play a central role in the healing. The mission developed by DMH, CSP, and the Boston Public Schools was to provide an organized response infrastructure at the neighborhood level for children and youth exposed to traumatic incidents and continuous threats of violence or adverse childhood experiences (ACEs). This mission called for a youth-focused trauma response service that could provide immediate, effective, and efficient intervention by adult caregivers in neighborhoods feeling the impact.

During the first six months of the grant, the CSP began working with the Boston Public Schools superintendent and his leadership team along with seven Boston community-based mental health agencies. In early September of 1997, CSP launched its first training to credential child trauma clinicians to respond to traumatic incidents in Boston, credentialing sixty-seven community-based clinicians with diverse cultural and linguistic backgrounds. As the CSP plans and protocols for responding to major threats and traumatic incidents having an impact on youth were further developed, the program began to implement responses. This included working closely, usually for two to three weeks, with Boston youth after their exposure to sudden violent deaths and drug overdoses. In late December 1996, these youth had informed us that there were three HUD–Boston Housing developments in which large numbers of youth were overdosing and attempting suicide. By early December of 1997, CSP had completed visits to all three housing developments. The situation was far worse than the reports from the streets had described and far worse than one could ever possibly imagine without having seen it firsthand. Dozens of youth were overdosing on heroin, cocaine, and prescription drugs—overdosing in their apartments, in the hallways, on the rooftops, in the alleyways. Hundreds of younger children were witnessing these overdoses on an hourly basis. And kids, between the ages of fourteen and twenty, were beginning to die, first from lethal overdoses and then by suicide.

Immediately CSP and DMH began working very closely with the Housing Authority, the mayor, and the neighborhood leaders, all of whom gave endless hours without hesitation in an attempt to quell the violence against self. Over the next nine months more than one child per month took his or her own life; dozens of youth attempted suicide; dozens of youth continued overdosing; more than one hundred youth were hospitalized. Thousands of youth attended funerals and witnessed the casket roll down the aisle and then later, at the cemetery, be lowered into the ground. No form of expert assistance appeared to slow the pace of self-destruction. CSP implemented a community-based training to credential youth trauma responders among the local adults who worked most closely with the neighborhood youth. Forty-seven neighborhood adults were given twenty hours of rigorous training and practice in how to respond to youth survivors, those who had witnessed a suicide or were in some other way connected with the person attempting or completing suicide.

In the last two hours of the training, CSP was paged by the police with the information that another child, a sixteen-year-old from the neighborhood, had successfully completed suicide. I was in the training room with others from CSP; each trainee in the room knew this child. Each one of us hung our head in silence, and in fear. This was the seventh kid in less than four months. After a brief break we reassembled and built our response plan for the first seventy-two hours, which included immediate reconnaissance to verify the identity of the decedent, the location of the body, the official cause of death, and the identities of any first-circle survivors (eyewitness to the suicide, decedent's siblings, current and recent lovers of the decedent, decedent's closest friends) and any second- and third-circle survivors (decedent's classmates and associates).

In the room were newly credentialed trainees who worked for the local police district, and they were assigned to handle communication with the coroner to verify cause of death prior to the implementation of our response, and to plan afternoon and evening street patrols to decrease street-corner suicide memorials (to lessen the chance that other children would attempt to copy the suicide). In the room were trainees who knew the decedent's parents, and they were assigned to proceed immediately to the hospital emergency room to work with the parents in developing a safety plan for the next twelve hours (arranging support for the parents during the process of identifying their child's body, planning how to take care of their traumatic stress response physiology, planning how to maintain their sleep and hydration, and offering assistance in contacting the parents' primary care doctor to ensure medical stabilization). In the room were ER nurses, who were assigned to proceed immediately to the emergency room and block all visits and body viewing from the decedent's friends, set up a hospital holding area for the decedent's friends, and tell these friends where our defusing meeting would be held. In the room were trainees who were the executive director and program director of the local neighborhood community center and who knew literally every survivor friend of the decedent; they were assigned to set up the community center for the orientation and defusing meeting and an after-meeting vigil and dinner.

In the room were Boston Public School student support personnel from the impacted neighborhood, who were assigned to coordinate communications with all school staff impacted by the suicide and to develop safety plans and school-based responses for the following day. In the room were members of the local faith based community, who were assigned to brief the clergy handling the funeral about the incident and set up an appointment for CSP to work with the primary cleric regarding the funeral ritual in order to decrease potential suicide contagion mechanisms. In the room were local mental health clinicians, who were assigned to cover the community center, both inside and outside and its surrounding streets, during the orientation and defusing meeting in order to provide one-to-one contact with any youth survivor who could not tolerate the group meeting and to make an acute level of care assessment if necessary.

In the room were employees of the local funeral homes, who were assigned to work with the family and our team to make sure we had permission from the family and the funeral director to be present at the wake to support youth survivors as they paid their respects and said goodbye. In the room were local neighbors who worked for the Mayor's Office and who were assigned to manage the scheduling changes in city-owned recreation spaces in order to provide additional meeting and recreation space for the youth survivors over the next two weeks. In the room were local heroes whose courage and patience and faith remains unsurpassed, who could have continued their weeping and who might have drifted into that dreaded numb and isolated space after hearing that yet another one of their neighborhood children had taken his own life. But instead they allowed themselves to go into an appraisal state, neither fighting, fleeing, nor freezing but rather listening carefully and offering advice carefully and immediately using their newly learned skills *to act*, to offer protection and safety, compassion and leadership to the youth survivors.

Within one hour of receiving the police page, the reconnaissance was completed, and all forty-seven trainees were stationed at their assignments. By now the news of the suicide had begun to spread rapidly through the small community. Close and not-so-close friends of the sixteen-year-old decedent literally ran to the ER and were received by adults whom they knew; carrying out our agreed-upon protocol, the ER nurses comforted these youth, but diverted them from viewing their best friend's body, no matter how they pleaded. Other survivors had heard that the orientation and defusing meeting would be held at the local community center, and they began arriving singly, in pairs, and in groups. Within ninety minutes of our receiving the police page, over sixty kids, mostly youth between fourteen and twenty, arrived at the community center. CSP had twenty newly trained responders on scene.

As these youth approached the community center, running, stumbling, screaming, and yelling, they exhibited the fight, flight, and freeze responses—all at the same time and all in an attempt to regain some control, some sense of protection, some sense of cause. They were throwing themselves against the walls and the sidewalks, cursing and hugging each other, literally tearing at their hair and hands, cursing us, hugging us, sobbing in our arms and then violently pushing us away. Seven young friends dead in four months. The twenty newly trained responders, knowing each of these kids by name and temperament, stood in appraisal, their eyes reflecting sadness and anger but also compassion, resolve, and courage. This community network was definitely stronger than the sum of its parts. At this moment I knew I was part of CSP's golden rule, being carried to safety by that golden rule: those most impacted play the central role.

After thirty minutes of running and pacing and sobbing, about fifty-four of the kids were able to enter the space we had arranged into a circle and begin to calm their breathing and attempt to listen. We gave a slow and soft recitation of the facts as we knew them and of the rumors as we had heard them, gently insisting that our survivor group be careful to distinguish between the two. We continued our orientation, a structured protocol that orients group members, in their language and at their level, to the traumatic incident or threat event specifics and the neurophysiology of the traumatic stress response. Orientations always precede any type of event processing as they are designed to decrease threat detection behaviors and engage safety-seeking behaviors as well as to screen for those group members who cannot tolerate the group process or who are so upset and aroused that they need acute stabilization.

During this orientation there were continued interruptions by group members who were alternately laughing and crying or jumping up and running from the room. Every time a group member ran from the room, one of our newly trained staff would run with him or her, even if it meant running down the sidewalk with the youth until he or she slowed and allowed himself or herself to be calmed. We would then do some one-to-one work with these youth if they so desired, or remain in silence with them if that was their wish, and then, when they were ready, walk them back to the group and help them rejoin. No matter how many times these youth left the group, they were welcomed back.

By the time we were ready to begin the defusing or processing portion of the group intervention nearly all the fifty-four kids were in attendance. All fifty-four ended up speaking during the two hours it took to complete the defusing. CSP directed the content toward identifying resources that could lead to safety and then worked on concretizing actual safety plans for individuals, couples, and small groups. Safety plans were designed by the kids, with our stewardship, to help them cope with their own physical and mental states so that they would engage in as few health-risk behaviors as possible. This is usually accomplished by allowing kids to come up with action plans that involve positive self-care practices they have engaged in successfully before, such as going for walks or working out with friends, listening to or playing music, creating art or writing in journals, making sure not to spend too much time alone, talking with respected elders, and protecting sleep and healthy eating habits.

After the defusing officially ended food was prepared, and all staff and kids had a meal together. At this point many kids were able to spend some extended private time with adults they knew and trusted. Youth who were not planning to go home that night were guided and assisted to call their parents or guardians and notify them of their plans. By this time it was some five hours after receiving the police page. The community center was to remain open until 10 P.M. for those kids who wanted to stay, but they were all encouraged to get to their homes and follow their self-care and safety plans. The last of the kids left by 8 P.M. It is important to note here that we never once told them that "time would heal," that they would "recover eventually." In fact we never told them what they should *not* do, including abusing substances, but rather we gathered information from them about what adaptational responses had already worked for them to keep them safe in the face of threat, and we reinforced their adaptive coping strategies. If they did not have any existing positive coping strategies, we made sure to support other group members in helping them build positive strategies.

Prior to leaving, we staff members held an exit meeting to discuss how each of us was doing, what our own safety plans would be, and what protocols would be used to provide appropriate support during the funeral service. About fifteen of the same staff that had worked the community center volunteered to work the wake and the funeral.

At the funeral the youth survivors tended to immediately gravitate toward these staff when they began to sob or pace or feel out of control. Having prepared counseling rooms with water and tissues, the staff positioned themselves both inside and outside the funeral home and church. Certain staff were stationed near the open casket to "catch" those kids who were fainting and get them seated against a wall, use ammonia capsules to revive them, hydrate them, and support them in getting back to the wake or funeral if they so wished or to the counseling rooms to rest or engage in one-to-one counseling.

This experience reinforced for the CSP staff just how powerful, safe, and effective the community-based trauma response model is, and we decided it was important to build similar capacities in the other fourteen neighborhoods of Boston. This capacity building for youth trauma response has been intended to address a wide spectrum of traumas, including large-scale threat events, such as the suicide cluster just described or the recent terrifying events of September 11, 2001, which cause high mortality rates but happen very rarely (high-impact–low-incidence events). But most important, the trauma response network system that is described in the following section has been built and maintained to consistently address the threat and terror experienced by individual youth during their regular waking hours. These events may be referred to as low-impact–high-incidence (meaning that they have a low mortality rate but happen frequently). This type of incident is unfortunately given little attention and continues to increase across our nation and in many parts of the world. Presently there are no reliable methods to measure the longitudinal impact of such daily events, but we do have strong evidence from the ACE study and epidemiological studies of the prevalence of PTSD to support the notion that these low-impact–high-incidence events produce significant developmental delays and long-term emotional, cognitive, physical, and social impairments.

Network building

Over the next seven years CSP built a collaborative youth *trauma response network* (TRN) for each neighborhood in Boston. This network not only provides direct intervention during critical incidents across the city, but also is part of a broad training and outreach program designed so that community members who are affected by threatening events may play a central role in the healing of their own neighborhoods. Lessons learned from this network building include how to best involve communities in their own recovery when critical incidents or threat events occur and how to provide supportive psychoeducational resources for exposed and impacted youth. One of the most valuable products developed through this work is the multimodal, Classroom-Based Intervention described in Chapter Three.

The network building that has taken place during these seven years has increasingly engaged more and more community partners who have specialized knowledge of different local neighborhood youth populations, such as the staffs of gay, lesbian, bisexual, and transgender youth organizations and the staffs managing safe house residences for youth attempting to sever their ties with a violent gang. Community partners have been selected and recruited from those agencies that have the most direct access to the least-resourced youth. These have included the community development, public health, education, youth development, and law enforcement entities shown in the following list, who are united around concern for youth health and emotional recovery in the face of threat:

Boston Public Schools: for example, Student Support Services, the Superintendent's Office and Leadership Team, and the Public Safety Department.

Municipal agencies: for example, the Mayor's Office of Health and Human Services, the Office of Neighborhood Services, community centers, the Youth Cleanup Corps, employee assistance programs, the Department of Youth Services, and the Department of Social Services

Community-based organizations: for example, youth-serving organizations such as Boys and Girls Clubs, Youth Worker Alliances, and neighborhood community centers

Health agencies: for example, public health commissions and state departments of public health, especially adolescent violence prevention and intentional injury units

Medical services: for example, Emergency Medical Services and Behavioral Health Emergency Response Teams, Divisions of Medical Assistance (Medicaid)

Housing authority: for example, HUD-Boston Housing Authority Management Teams, tenant task forces, family development directors, the HUD police, and the Youth Workers Program in the Community Initiatives Department

Law enforcement: for example, the chief Probation Department, the Juvenile Court judges, and the Municipal Police Department, including specialty units such as the Violence Gang Unit, Domestic Violence Unit, Sexual Assault Unit, Civil Disorders Unit (First Amendment Violations), Hostage Negotiating Unit, and police social workers unit

Faith community: for example, the 10 Point Coalition-Clergy Consortium; the Black Ministerial Alliance-Clergy Consortium; God's Posse-Violent Gang Involved Youth Christian Consortium; the New Covenant Christian Center; the Catholic Charities, Archdiocese of Boston; and others among Boston's most respected faith-based community leadership organizations

These organizations provide a broad-based and interdisciplinary coalition that operates throughout Boston neighborhoods; so when a critical incident occurs that affects Boston youth, the Community Services Program has immediate access to a network of supports.

CSP and its community partners have developed and currently manage an extensive youth violence and trauma response network for the city of Boston and surrounding neighborhood communities, covering over 100,000 urban youth. CSP maintains a 365/24/7 electronic pager support service so it can respond to a broad range of traumatic events. Our pager system is connected to the municipal mayoral and police alert systems, the state emergency management systems, and the International American Red Cross Alert System, and it can be accessed by 450 Boston-based, licensed clinical mental health youth trauma specialists; 480 Boston Public Schools and Boston parochial school non-classroom-based employees; and over 950 Boston-based, community-based professionals working in varying capacities with youth. Each of these credentialed TRN members responds daily to youth violence, separation, loss, and ongoing traumatic incidents occurring in Boston and its surrounding communities. The events most frequently responded to by our teams include domestic violence with spousal homicide, youth homicide, youth suicide attempts and completions, multiple-fatality car accidents, multiple-fatality school bus accidents, sudden death of a student due to medical anomaly, First Amendment violations, gang violence and nonfatal penetrating wounds, and hostage takings (in some cases involving homicide and suicide). When a traumatic event or other threat event occurs or is expected to occur, any number of network partners may choose to page us, requesting either (1) case consultation, case management, and ongoing case supervision or (2) on-scene direct care services, as outlined in detail later.

The credentialing process for the TRN is the cornerstone of the program with respect to implementing incident-specific protocols and maintaining quality assurance. In order to become a credentialed TRN member, individuals must first apply for acceptance into our basic training program by submitting their résumés and references. We then conduct an interview with each candidate. If accepted, candidates must successfully complete the twenty-hour basic training, fourteen hours of which is actual practice of intervention techniques with close observation by two instructors. Once they are TRN members, they must adhere to these basic rules of conduct: (1) all responses remain confidential and no medical records are kept, (2) never do a response alone, and never go to the scene without being invited and knowing whom to report to, (3) complete full reconnaissance prior to beginning any intervention, (4) always use the standardized incident-specific protocols as defined by the basic and advanced training modules, (5) always use basic methodologies for doing no harm during interventions, and (6) be prepared to be debriefed after being on-scene, as part of a defined self-care plan to reduce the potential for vicarious trauma or compassion fatigue. Each credentialed TRN member must complete continuing education by attending a minimum of four eight-hour advanced trainings per year, conducted by the CSP senior training staff. Advanced training addresses these topics: traumatic incident orientations; suicide and homicide; traumatic stress interventions for pre-K and early elementary children; the process of normal grief; traumatic grief and complicated grief; psychological process debriefings for eyewitnesses; traumatic stress interventions and expressive therapy; traumatic stress interventions and cognitive behavioral therapy; ethnocultural variables in traumatic stress responses; developmental pathways and the impact of traumatic stress; women and children exposed to armed conflict: exposure scenarios and intervention strategies; intervention techniques for youth exposed to First Amendment violations; roots of school violence; interventions for youth exposed to terrorist attacks; and developmentally specific stress inoculation protocols.

In order to respond to a traumatic incident or threat event effectively, and especially to ensure that no harm is done during the intervention, it is imperative that any youth trauma response team understands that traumatic stress reactions and impact scenarios will vary enormously, both for the individual and the community, depending on the incident specifics (the type of threat event). So professional credentialing must include advanced training in how to conduct incident-specific reconnaissance, incident-specific contagion containment protocols, and incident-specific prevention, intervention, and postvention protocols. It is not within the scope of this volume to outline the step-by-step details of each of these protocols, which are explicated elsewhere,[2] but it is important for the youth interventionist to understand the domain that applies to each specific incident, as follows:

Abusive behavior incident

Disruptive student in the classroom
Hate crimes
Life-threatening substance abuse
Sexual abuse of student

Sexual harassment of student
Student self-mutilation—cutting

Fatal incident

Motor vehicle accident with student fatality
Student placed on life-support machine
Sudden death of staff
Sudden death of student
Suicide completion

Medical threat

Communicable disease exposure
Environmental hazard exposure
Food poisoning, unintentional toxin ingestion
School bus accident

Missing person incident

Abduction of student
Missing student or missing teacher

Threats and acts of violence

Bomb explosion
Bomb threat
Physical attacks (with weapon or without weapon—bullying)
Suicide attempt
Student body riot
Verbal and physical threats (with weapon or without weapon)
Violent gang conflict

School operations threat

Earthquake
False fire alarm
Fire at school
Hurricane
Severe flooding

Telephone, fax, or Internet abuse
Tornado
Unauthorized visitor on school premises

Terrorism threat

CBRNE attack (chemical, biological, radiological, nuclear, and
  high-yield explosives)
Ongoing armed conflict in Middle East
Ongoing urban armed conflict
Psychological warfare

As this list might indicate, the potential threat scenarios for youth
exposed to one or more of these traumatic incidents must be handled
in a carefully structured manner. Problems arising from such events
are just too complex to be dealt with by one agency, one method, or
one group of experts. It is essential to put together a carefully selected
network that can manage complex responses at the local level, which
ultimately means using local expertise to (1) identify those most
impacted; (2) identify those most resilient; (3) identify the closest,
least expensive, most appropriate recovery resources; and (4) follow
through on the long-range response after the experts, the media, and
the attention grabbers have left the scene. Once this local expertise
has been identified and *their* needs assessed and their training customized to meet their needs, a continuum of care can be designed for
that particular neighborhood so that this network can respond pro-
fessionally to a range of threat events.

TRN intervention methods

In the first twenty-four to forty-eight hours after a critical incident,
the work of the TRN consists of stabilization. Simply put, stabilization means that the individual or group is removed from the
impacted environment (*ground zero*) and given enough support and
containment to feel truly out of danger. A spectrum of interven-

tions may then be implemented, tailored to the needs of the particular community and the particular event.[3]

Usually, within twenty-four hours, our TRN will offer, if invited, the following:

Traumatic incident orientations: augmenting and supporting normal recovery of normal kids having normal reactions over a normal period of time to highly abnormal and violent events in their lives and the lives of their friends

Traumatic incident management: targeting the absolute reduction of prolonged traumatic stress responses in youth survivors after critical incidents have occurred (that is, sudden and violent death, including suicide; nonfatal penetrating wounds; First Amendment violations; being an eyewitness to drugs and weapons trafficking; or other violence contagion events).

The spectrum of interventions applied during a critical incident ranges from individual crisis or medical intervention to acute psychiatric hospitalization. These interventions may also include demobilization (removing the impacted population from the impact zone and providing them an environment in which they can actively disengage from the survival mode), traumatic incident management (which includes group interventions to review stress responses and construct safety plans), and referral for ongoing outpatient therapy or faith-based counseling.

Assessment of functioning

In our assessment of function, we conduct a *trauma status exam* to determine whether affected teens are experiencing unusually heightened arousal or dissociation, intrusive thoughts, flashbacks or nightmares, numbing, or agitation. This helps us assess the appropriateness of group versus individual interventions. The typical contraindications for group intervention are bizarre behavior, inability to contain emotions; extreme motor agitation; extreme dissociation (being nonverbal, spaced out, or unresponsive or having a "1,000-mile stare"), extreme aggression, or extreme numbing.

Individual crisis intervention

When assessing the need for individual crisis intervention, we first address safety issues: Is there a medical or psychological emergency, or are there other safety issues that require immediate professional attention? When interventions are conducted, the trauma response personnel identify appropriately private and calm settings. In each session, we follow a typical protocol:

- First, remind the youth we are working with that very bad things do happen to good people.
- Discuss what happened, using a low-key elicitation of the event's narrative, without deep probing.
- Provide concrete information to explain that the youth's disturbing reactions are perfectly normal (normalization), and offer additional psychosocial education about trauma and recovery.
- Assist the youth with resource identification (who and what can he or she use for support) and self-care planning.
- Assess the youth for further referral: for example, to a primary care physician, mental health clinic or provider, substance abuse treatment center, clergy, local support groups, or legal aid.

Information and education sessions

We provide more general information or psychoeducational sessions to individuals and groups who were not directly involved in the incident but are in need of some support. This includes offering orientation sessions that provide appropriate information about what happened, about coping and providing support to others, about critical incident services available, and about ways of using the community network of resources to augment support.

Response continuum

CSP staff and TRN personnel are involved in developing a response continuum, or triage system, for each critical incident. The tasks involved include

• *Identifying and supporting youth affected by the incident.* This requires identifying the youth who had primary exposure (eyewitness or close connection to event), secondary exposure (bystander or other connection to incident), and tertiary exposure (not directly involved, but still at risk for trauma). Different levels of exposure require different intensities of intervention, and competent services require developmental and ethnocultural perspectives.

• *Identifying and working with community partners and existing resources.* This means establishing an *asset map* of local agencies—such as community organizations, schools, city departments, faith organizations, and mental health agencies—that can play an important role in youth recovery. At the trauma center we include our own standardized training and credentialing process as a resource.

• *Finding out what happened.* This requires getting a reliable incident narrative, finding out what services are already being delivered, and gaining information about victims, eyewitnesses, and the cause of harm or death. If there is a decedent, we must take religious and cultural considerations into account as we assist with recovery support and funeral planning.

• *Management of the event site.* This means establishing a principal information officer and a communication center. Misinformation or partial information is common during a critical incident, so communication must be managed well. It is also necessary to establish meeting places for impacted youth, parents, and staff and to begin setting up psychoeducational meetings and interventions.

• *Stabilization.* This involves one-on-one interventions, group orientations, and defusings, and referrals for additional mental health or support services for those who are not able to feel safe once the event is over.

• *Coping and resource identification (debriefing).* This requires having critical incident services for families, following up on referrals, and having long-term follow-up methods such as survivor groups, individual services, and postcritical incident seminars. Conducting prevention efforts also falls under this general heading. These efforts may include violence management and prevention programs for schools or work sites; safety protocols such as evacuation plans, notification of first responders, a threat of violence policy and response procedures; crisis management planning; and identification of positive coping skills.

Critical incident intervention design

Today we in America may live in the most violent society in the world. Dahlberg cites the following risk factors that lead to violence: (1) early onset of aggressive behaviors in childhood, (2) deficits in social problem-solving skills, (3) exposure to violence, (4) negative peer influences, and (5) poor family functioning, which lowers a child's ability to problem solve.[4] Without a strong sense of community, our children manifest a lack of connection with their environment and their lost sense of community through acts of violence. Children living out their formative years beneath the poverty level are at greater risk of experiencing developmental delays. In addition, these children are often exposed to greater levels of traumatic material than are other children. These same children, displaying short attention spans or lack of interest, are routinely diagnosed with attention deficit disorder (ADD) or attention deficit hyperactivity disorder (ADHD) and are medicated. This is particularly true for boys. Frustrated, communities attempt to intervene when their symptoms are most severe, usually during adolescence.

The CSP service summaries for the last seven years reflect the profound lessons of building our type of community network to address some of the community's most painful experiences. When CSP first entered the HUD–Boston Housing developments we had no idea what we were getting into. We had no idea how far-reaching the negative effects of traumatic incidents and ongoing threat events can be for youth, especially underresourced youth. What we did learn, thanks to the local heroes, is that the most effective service delivery must be accomplished by those who know the youth the best, which will usually mean those adults who will be impacted most deeply by the sudden, violent loss of their neighborhood youth. In considering the design and implementation of a youth trauma response network, we learned to never underestimate the leadership, skills, and consistent courage of our local partners, and to make sure they are an integral part of our network needs assessment and design from the beginning. This has helped us to foster the best relationships we can with those youth most at risk and those youth most capable of taking on leadership roles in the community.

Notes

1. Dahlberg, L. L. (1998). Youth violence in the United States: Major trends, risk factors, and prevention approaches. *American Journal of Preventive Medicine, 14*(4), 259–272.

2. Macy, R. D. (2000). *PLANet: An Internet based school crisis plan manager, primary content provider.* King of Prussia, PA: Strohl Systems. Retrieved from www.schools.planetstrohl.com 2000.

3. Giannantonio, M. (Ed.). (2003). Roger Solomon and Robert D. Macy. In *Psicotraumatologia e psicologia dell'emergenza.* Salerno: Ecomind.

4. Dahlberg (1998).

ROBERT D. MACY *is executive director, the Center for Trauma Psychology; codirector, National Center for Child Traumatic Stress Network-Category III; and director, Community Services, the Trauma Center-Boston. In collaboration with codirector Bessel van der Kolk, he is responsible for the Category III design, development, and service delivery management of the national initiative to research and treat child and adolescent posttraumatic stress disorders funded by the Substance Abuse and Mental Health Services Administration. Macy is also the director of psychosocial initiatives at the Trauma Center-Boston and founder of the Community Services Program, which manages the Metro Boston Trauma Response Network for Youth.*

The Classroom-Based Intervention emphasizes a specific theme each week to allow children to construct safe places to express their stories and develop coping strategies in a group environment.

3

Healing in familiar settings: Support for children and youth in the classroom and community

Robert D. Macy, Dicki Johnson Macy,
Steven I. Gross, Pamela Brighton

IN THE FALL of 1999, the Marmara region in central Turkey suffered two severe earthquakes (7.5 on the Richter scale) leaving more than 19,000 children and adults dead and over 100,000 people homeless. The earthquake zone covered over 30,000 square kilometers. As with any large-scale natural disaster, private and public sector assistance flooded in from many parts of the world. Many trauma experts arrived in different parts of the impact zone to assist with assessment and psychological triage. Standard trauma response protocols for youth included "getting them back to school, back to their routines." This of course made sense, especially because many of these children were now homeless, living in tent cities, and so being in school during the day at least offered them some structure and safety.

Between the first and second earthquakes, Macy and the Center for Trauma Psychology received a call from Atle Dyregrov,

NEW DIRECTIONS FOR YOUTH DEVELOPMENT, NO. 98, SUMMER 2003 © WILEY PERIODICALS, INC.

director of the Center for Crisis Psychology in Norway, asking if we would be willing to come to Turkey and "take a look" at the youth in their schools and the tent cities. Reports from the Turkish Ministry of Health, Ministry of Education, and Ministry of Social Work indicated that youth, even though back in school, "were not doing very well." Youth risk behaviors normally quite foreign to the Turkish youth culture were beginning to escalate, and teachers and parents were unable to decrease these behaviors or "control" the children. Reported reactions and behaviors included significantly increased targeted aggression among elementary and secondary students and among siblings; enuresis among elementary and middle school students; sleep disturbance among all ages; extreme fear of the dark and of enclosed spaces among all ages; intense hypervigilance among all ages in anticipation of the "next earthquake"; marked decrease in ability to concentrate, focus, memorize, or take pleasure in safe and calm play among all ages; a precipitous falloff in classroom performance and academic achievement for elementary, middle, and high school students; marked disregard and disrespect toward teachers and parents as well as truancy among middle and high school students, behaviors normally not exhibited or tolerated in Turkey; substance abuse, including cigarette and alcohol intake and "huffing," or inhalant use, among high school students, also a stark deviation from the pre-earthquake norm; and multiple variations of high-risk play among all ages, including some reports of self-destructive behaviors and suicide attempts, again far from the norm for Turkey and for Muslim cultures.

The reports seemed to verify what we had learned from our youth trauma response work in the United States: traumatic incidents and ongoing threat events (the aftershocks from the earthquakes lasted for four months and registered as high as 4 and 5 on the Richter scale) can cause high levels of sustained autonomic dysregulation among exposed youth. Yet we did not necessarily view these behaviors as pathogenic or maladaptive but rather as an adaptational process engaged in by the impacted youth to regain some control over their lives. We needed to see these kids and their environments firsthand, and we needed to talk to the local experts. Our hunch was that the local experts would know what to do with their own children if we could calm the adult caregivers down and assist them with safety-seeking and attachment navigation. While we were in the air traveling toward Turkey the second earthquake occurred. Needless to say the Turkish youth were correct: there were more earthquakes coming and they were "justified" in their behaviors.

After visiting with various ministers and nongovernmental organization (NGO) staff we were able to go into the field and take a look at the youth and their environments. We visited schools and spoke with principals, teachers, and students—the true experts on what the real threats were and what might be needed to reclaim safety. Some number of these folks pleaded with us: "Please, no more expert psychological assessments for us and our kids— we know that we are disturbed. . . . we just went through an earthquake. . . . we want to know what to do about it . . . no one is feeling safe and everyone is angry." We visited hospitals and spoke with doctors, nurses, and psychiatrists; we visited homes and spoke with surviving relatives—the parents, sons and daughters, aunts and uncles. We visited broken, shattered villages and spoke with survivors in the streets and shops and restaurants. They told us of their pain, their sudden violent losses, their frightening stories of en-trapment under the rubble, and they told us of their resolve to rebuild. The eyes of many seemed saddened and fearful, lost and isolated. The Turks are brave, strong, and bright people. They adore and dote on their children. Much of their sadness, indeed most of their sadness, appeared to be related to the threat exposures their children had endured. The adults, parents, teachers, administrators, and service providers were desperately insistent on knowing what to do for their children in order to return them to normal, to help them stop wetting their beds, stop crying in the darkness, stop sleeping in their parents' bed after ten years of sleeping alone, stop failing "on purpose" in school.

And then we visited one of the largest tent cities. The lead author of this chapter reports his experiences there:

It was about an hour before dusk. As we walked in through the security gate I saw hundreds of tent tops and hundreds of adults beginning to prepare their suppers and talking in quiet tones in small groups as the cook pots boiled and the smoke rose up above the tent tops. I was immediately struck by two things: the way the rhythm of life continues, seemingly no matter the adverse circumstances, and . . . the fact that there was an absolutely gorgeous, expensive, brand-new playground, the nicest playground I have ever seen, without one child playing on it. In fact, as I began to look around for the kids, I did not see any youth in sight other than babies still in the arms of their mothers. But I could hear them. I wanted to walk around in the tent city by myself, essentially to find out where the kids were hanging out and what they were up to, but my guides and security were at first hesitant to let me wander on my own. Once I convinced them that I would be careful and respectful, I headed off in the direction of the kids' voices.

At the far end of the tent city, diagonally opposite the entrance, as far away from the beautiful playground as possible, a group of at least 150 children were intensely engaged in their "play." These kids ranged in age from perhaps six years old to twenty years old. They had taken the wooden pallets the tents had arrived on and had stacked them, fifteen or twenty pallets high, to create rickety wooden towers swaying some twelve to fifteen feet above the ground. Children were standing in line, most of them silently, awaiting their turn to climb up the swaying towers and jump from the top of one tower to another, freezing as they landed so as not to topple the tower over. Apparently you "won" if you did not make the tower fall down. There were six-year-old children doing this, . . . over and over again, . . . their eyes wide not with joyful excitement but with a strange mix of fear and numbness, as if they were robots. Suddenly I realized I was witnessing their actual earthquake experience, reenacted right in front of me. Had I not once stood in the doorways of the HUD–Boston Housing developments and been brought to safety by the local heroes there, I would not have withstood this witnessing with any great strength or insight.

Our intervention guides, our supervisors, were right in front of me. They were doing what they knew how to do best—play, playing hard in order to keep their fears at a distance. Playing *now*, in the moment, at great risk to themselves, because perhaps they no longer sensed their future— fighting, fleeing, and freezing all at the same time, their capacity for appraisal muted. They had actually turned their traumatic stress response into a game—these little geniuses—in a dangerous attempt to adapt to a world that no longer provided control. These youth were reliving the earthquake, so that with extreme practice they could get very good at being in earthquakes, perhaps even good enough to be in control during the next earthquake, and they had nothing to lose because of course there would be another earthquake. No need to play at the playground, no time to waste—life was too short. These behaviors provided the essential key for what I needed to do with them next, given the existing knowledge of the impact of trauma on development and the established protocols from the Boston-based CSP work. The youth earthquake survivors were rapidly becoming experts on threat detection. In their sincere efforts to make sure that they could be in control when the next threat occurred, they had completely given up safety seeking and thus were not interested in or particularly motivated to seek soothing attachments that might calm their arousal, that might give them permission to feel safe, if even for just ten seconds.

So I went to get my translator, and we followed a couple of kids to their tents and had dinner with them. I convinced them to meet me after dinner at the playground playhouse with whichever friends they might choose. When they arrived I had set up a long bench, with cushions on the floor on each side of the bench. On top of the bench I had placed about a dozen glasses filled halfway with water. I had noticed in the earthquake zone that adults kept a half-filled glass of water on top of their desks or computers, which provided them with a primitive seismographic reading to determine if any shaking they were experiencing was just a construction truck going by, in which case the water did not shake, or if the shaking was indeed another earthquake or large aftershock, in which case the water in the glass would jiggle noticeably. All . . . the kids knew of this technique.

As the kids came into the play space I greeted them gently and asked if they would be comfortable sitting on the cushions. Most of them declined to sit; they were wary but curious. After brief introductions all around I thanked them for letting me be with them and I thanked them for trusting my Turkish colleagues and me. I then asked them if they could see the water glasses on the bench. They said yes. I asked them if they could see whether the water was moving or not. Complete silence. Some of them squinted; some of them came close to the bench and squatted, examining the water with great care. Were they seeking threat or safety? They were seeking . . . both at the same time, a major change from their tower play and the beginning of a transition. Notice I did not ask them whether they *thought* the water was moving. We were interested in having them tell us what they actually saw, what they actually felt, what their bodies told them. After several minutes they all decided, as a group, that the water was not moving. So I asked them to consider that if the water was not moving, could they agree that at this moment there was no earthquake happening. It appeared to me that they were wondering if it was a trick question. I continued to gently remind them to trust their eyes and bodies and make sure the water was not moving. Again, as a group they determined that because the water was not moving an earthquake could not be happening.

Once this was agreed upon I "went for" the leap of faith. I asked them next, "Since you all agree that the water is not moving and therefore you all agree that there is no earthquake happening right now, could we all also agree that we are safe, at least in this moment, that we will be safe, say for the next ten seconds. . . . keep your eyes on the water and I will count to ten." Eyes focused intensely on the water, shoulders beginning to drop, some knees beginning to bend slightly, breathing becoming audible and deepened. Fight, flight, and freeze were diminishing; appraisal was taking hold in the service of safety seeking. As I reached the number ten the kids all sighed, and they looked so proud of themselves and so relieved. We all smiled at each other in silence. I said, "Do you want to try to get to twenty? . . . Can we all feel safe, as long as the water is not moving, for twenty seconds?" They were eager to "try" and so they did and so we began the process of building safety, in small increments, until they could feel safe for longer periods of time. These experts had taught me it is better to add safety-seeking practice than to interrupt and scorn threat detection behaviors.

Using classroom-based intervention in Turkey

In the end the Turkish ministries, their NGO partners, and the United Nations agency UNICEF asked us to "work" with some 100,000 earthquake exposed youth, "as soon as possible." We knew that the only possibility of accomplishing such a mission was to allow those adults most impacted by the earthquakes an opportunity to play a central role in the design and implementation of the resolution and recovery interventions. We brought together our core staff from the Center for Trauma Psychology and, using our materials from the Boston programs and the trauma response incident-specific protocols, we designed a fifteen-session template for a classroom-based intervention, which has since become known as the CBI. This template was then reviewed and customized for the Turkish culture and the Ministry of Education.

We wanted this intervention to be conducted in the classrooms in order to (1) normalize the intervention activities so children would not be stigmatized by participating, (2) normalize the CBI content as approved curricula for the school so the principal and teachers would approve and support the work, (3) embed the CBI safety-seeking practice sessions in the regular school day curriculum so that the traumatic stress reduction work became part of the "normal" day for kids . . . ("we have math, then science, then CBI, and then recess"), and (4) allow teachers and parents to receive collateral benefits from the new learning that takes place during the CBI and allow the adult caregivers to have the experience of a significant calming effect on the youth in an approved safe space and accepted educational environment—the school and the classroom.

The CBI used in Turkey was a carefully planned, developmentally specific, psychoeducational intervention involving a series of repetitive and highly structured activities aimed at supporting children to sustain a normal recovery over a normal period of time after highly stressful and possibly life-threatening events, such as the two Turkish earthquakes. In addition, the CBI targeted the reduction of those traumatic stress sequelae that might support the development or maintenance of PTSD. In order to identify and sustain normal recovery processes in children who have been exposed to traumatic stressors, the CBI targeted the immediate reduction of posttraumatic stress reactions. The expected immediate results included a significant reduction in disturbances of sleep, digestion and elimination, focus and concentration, and peer and adult relationships and an increase in age-appropriate self-care and play behaviors, self-soothing, safety seeking, sense of self-control, sense of taking another's social perspective, self-esteem, and a sense of the future.

The CBI activities implemented in Turkey between December of 1999 and June 2000 for the schools affected by the Marmara earthquake involved eight regions and thirty-three schools. A total of 213 trained guidance counselors, trained by the Center for Trauma Psychology (CTP) core faculty, conducted the fifteen-session, twenty-hour CBI, working with 12,868 students for six weeks. All individuals who conducted the fifteen-session CBI over six weeks were required, first, to be certified and approved guidance counselors and then to complete, at a minimum, the basic CBI three-day training course conducted by CTP-trained trainers and to receive ongoing supervision from CTP senior faculty and Turkish licensed psychologists.

The CBI program, the exact components of which are discussed in detail later in this chapter, employed many proven methods for processing youth's often fragmented memories and physical fears surrounding the traumatic events of the earthquakes. These included psychological debriefing techniques; cognitive behavioral therapy, including stress inoculation techniques and classical human conditioning; therapeutic storytelling; movement and music therapy; silent storytelling, or art, therapy; and highly structured cooperative games, or play therapy.

The students' CBI groups met three times a week in one-hour classes. Each week emphasized a specific theme. Some of these themes were information, safety, and stabilization; awareness, control, and self-esteem; thoughts and reactions during the earthquake; thoughts and reactions during and after the earthquake; resource identification and coping skills; and resource installation and future safety planning. These themes were interrelated in such a way as to provide the children with an opportunity to slowly build safe places in which they could then express the story of their earthquake experiences while identifying present and future resources and coping strategies in a group environment.

The CBI for Turkey went through a systematic evaluation study designed to quantitatively assess the qualitative effectiveness of these interventions. The monitoring and evaluation design involved a preintervention and postintervention assessment and comparison with a waiting-list control group.

Over 28,000 youth participated in the CBI in the classrooms of the Turkish elementary and high schools in the disaster regions in the first fourteen months of the implementation. Study subjects numbered 115 children and 369 adolescents. They came from low-, moderate-, and high-impact earthquake zones. Wait-list control subjects numbered 83 children and 275 adolescents. The preliminary outcome data, using non-PTSD measures, indicate a significant decrease in distress indices (anxiety, depression, self-esteem, affect management) for the study children and adolescents as compared to matched wait-list controls.

Since the relatively large-scale success of the pilot project, the CBI has been conducted throughout most of the Turkish earthquake zone. Approximately some 55,000 youth have now completed the CBI, which has been conducted by over 1,000 trained interventionists. Requests for the CBI program have now come from a number of diverse international agencies, and the CBI is currently being conducted in the Middle East and is soon to be conducted in Nepal, Indonesia, and parts of Africa. It is also being conducted in urban centers in the United States.

Framework for healing

We developed the Classroom-Based Intervention program to provide a psychoeducational curriculum that can address the most critical needs of children and youth exposed to threat and terror. The CBI structure is adaptable to ages seven through nineteen. In this section we describe the main components of the framework. The CBI design is founded in long-standing, empirically derived practice models, such as cognitive behavior therapy and systematic desensitization. The CBI has now been tested in earthquake and other natural disaster zones and in the aftermath of armed conflicts and terrorists attacks such as that of September 11, 2001. We are, as mentioned, currently conducting this intervention work in the United States, Europe, and Asia and soon will be offering it in Africa. Our group consists of clinicians with training in either the arts or behavioral conditioning (MSWs and PhDs) and with specialized training backgrounds in youth trauma who partner with local teachers, youth counselors, and child-care workers to conduct this intensive classroom-based intervention aimed at stress inoculation against prospective threats as well as at stemming the traumatic effects of a threatening incident, supporting healing, and developing skills and techniques for recovering positive developmental trajectories.

Phase-oriented trauma treatment

Trauma-specific treatment involves a sequence of interventions to help students stabilize and return to the level of functioning they had before they were traumatized. The phases occur in a specific sequence, but all early phases are revisited and fully integrated into later phases. More specifically, the structure of this intervention program is based on proven models for decreasing arousal, hyper-vigilance, fear, and numbing in traumatized children after traumatic incidents and threat events. The design of the Classroom-Based Intervention program especially targets the students' need for safety, trust, and stabilization, the first phase of trauma treatment.

- *Safety* applies to the students' emotional and physical safety needs.
- *Trust* highlights the importance of reestablishing secure, consistent, and reliable social relationships.
- *Stabilization* refers to the need to stabilize students' responses and to begin healing the various disruptions in their physical, cognitive, emotional, and social functioning.

Two key concepts

The CBI work is based on the two key concepts that remain essential in all the youth trauma response work we have conducted:

1. An immediate, professional, psychological trauma-specific, short-term (six to eight weeks) response to children who have been exposed to life-threatening events significantly decreases the potential for overall negative effects from the terrifying experience. This includes significant decreases in sleep disturbance, nightmares, appetite disturbance, elimination disturbance, peer relationship disturbance, attention and learning disturbance, substance abuse, and self-destructive behaviors.

2. Traumatized survivors of life-threatening events are initially unable to coherently verbalize what happened to them or what they perceived happened to them during the disaster. In addition, children do not have the developed language capacity to process the traumatic experience verbally. We have found that other methods

of expression, such as silent storytelling, gross motor therapeutic play, and movement and music therapy, have been extraordinarily successful in helping trauma-exposed youth to process the negative experiences and return to normal functioning so that they can attend to teaching and learning.

These concepts underlie the way we approach each intervention, no matter what the threatening event. Although some differences in youth culture, age, and gender must be considered, our empirical research base has reinforced the validity of this paradigm.

Objectives of classroom-based psychosocial interventions

There are five main objectives of the fifteen-session CBI program, which can be conducted in school or after-school settings, camps, or other child and youth programs, although we recommend the classroom as the most stable and successful space to do the work.

Reduce the risk of maladaptation

One objective is to reduce the susceptibility of youth to developing intermediate and long-range maladaptive behaviors, acute traumatic stress disorders, and long-term mental illness and performance dysfunction.

Facilitate resiliency and return to normalcy

Another objective is to augment youth's immediate and sustained recovery from stress reactions to danger by supporting and increasing their resiliency, for instance their desire and ability to seek safety and meaningful attachments, thereby returning their lives to as close to normal as possible, so they can pay attention to teaching and learning in the classroom.

Following a traumatic event the child may perceive the world as undependable; as the child gains a positive sense of self through mastery and cooperative interaction with peers, his sense of safety, self-esteem, ability to solve problems, and self-control increase. He gains a more positive sense of the world around him and gains access to parts of himself that may be drawn upon for strength during difficult times. The development of resiliency and reconnection to the physical and social environments is most easily accomplished through the use of rhythm and creative activities that activate parts of the individual that are positive and constructive.

Facilitate empowerment and mastery

A third objective is to engage the students in various hands-on creative activities in order to actively involve them in self-expression, self-exploration, learning about their traumatic experiences, and practicing new ways of coping.

The use of movement, music, and creative activities in a consistent, predictable framework, featuring tasks the child is able to master (within an allotted time frame), facilitates a sense of empowerment. Mastering these tasks in the company of peers reduces her sense of isolation, encouraging a newfound sense of group empowerment.

Use a natural learning environment

To meet our fourth objective of using a natural learning environment, we encourage the use of settings such as camps or schools. This allows the interventions to take place during camp or school hours and be supervised by school staff so that the child will *normalize* his reaction to the traumatic experience. Learning in these familiar environments, being cared for by trusted adults, allows the camper or student to look upon their fearful experiences as learning experiences that they can safely study, give expression to, and understand.

Screen for high-risk youth

A final objective is to identify youth who are at the highest risk of developing prolonged acute stress disorder or chronic posttraumatic stress reactions and link these youth to appropriate psychosocial supports for additional follow-up care. This includes screening youth for health-risk behaviors such as smoking, drinking, and using other drugs; refusing to sleep and becoming sleep deprived; and driving recklessly. Although some of these activities may seem like typical "teenage rebellion," it is important to understand that many of the health-risk behaviors practiced by adolescents, especially after exposure to traumatic events, may be maladaptive coping strategies used in an attempt to lessen the negative effects of the traumatic stress response. Normally these maladaptive behaviors actually increase the negative effects of the traumatic exposure.

Methodologies of the intervention

We use a variety of methodologies in CBI, taking into account differences in both learning styles and coping strategies. We also tailor the specific activities in each methodology to be developmentally appropriate for each age group we work with (between seven and nineteen years of age). Prior to reviewing these methodologies, however, we present what we might refer to as the entrainment or conditioning paradigm for the CBI.

Trauma, experienced or imagined, has the potential to disconnect its victims from the energetic vortex of life's continuum, leaving isolated beings in its wake. A dynamic model of the universe understands life's continuum to be an energetic dialogue between opposing forces, evolving and dissolving, seeking balance and fulfillment. Because the state of isolation is one that opposes nature and its vitality, understanding the continuum concept may significantly affect those seeking psychological integration and physical health for individuals and their social matrixes. Remembering or reconnecting with the rhythms and patterns of nature may minimize this sense of isolation.

At some point in a life history "everyman," when disabled, disadvantaged, traumatized, or emotionally or physically needy, experiences some degree of isolation. Our society contributes to this sense of isolation, moving us away from nature's design and inspiration, teaching us to compete with each other and with the Universe, modeling competition as a winning style and being alone "at the top" as the coveted place. Somehow we have forgotten that living creatures, from the smallest strand of DNA to a human being, die when placed too long in isolation, physical, emotional, or imagined. On the other end of the spectrum, exaggerated togetherness, as experienced by children contained prematurely in the structure of "full-time day care," may be equally damaging. The healing process begins as we recognize the need for balance between solitude and affiliation. Moreover, solitude, integral to this vitality continuum, must be clearly differentiated from isolation, which is a static state and temporary, as permanent isolation is death.

The CBI is based on reclaiming and experiencing the vital rhythm that balances affiliation and solitude—within oneself, with the social and physical environment, and with the living universe. The use of rhythm (and music) is essential in making this effort toward balance. Rhythmicity is a universal phenomenon, observed in all life forms and therefore linking them all. Simply put, bringing this rhythmicity to one's awareness, moving one's body to a designated tempo, promotes connection, minimizing the experience of isolation.

The physical and symbolic circle, a component in nature's design, is one of the building blocks in the architecture of the CBI. In the physical circle everyone is equal and included; moving in a circular pattern is grounding and calming. Experiencing the continuum of life, the movement of breath in and out of the body, the cycles of the moon and the tides, of birth and death and spiritual return, is the metaphysical, symbolic circle. The circle is symbolic of integration; the integration of emotion, spirit, cognition, and the physical is what we seek in the healing process.

A circle defines the boundaries of inside and outside. As children strive to be included, the use of a physical map of inclusion (we use a brightly colored circle of cloth that we call a *parachute*) makes this goal accessible. If activities done on the parachute are consistent and cooperative, children begin to associate inclusion with positive, dependable experiences. The parachute or a circle of rope is a useful tool for encouraging the experience of bonding and connection without exaggerated intimacy. For example, children may move together to an established rhythm holding onto the circle of rope or circumference of the parachute. They are experiencing the joy of moving harmoniously together without touching each other. Children feel safe when adults construct boundaries for them; physical boundaries help children to contain their emotions, to feel under control, and to begin to explore and to understand their emotions. Their experience of the sensorial world is unfiltered; this may be experienced as chaos, exaggerated in the case of trauma. Mimicking and mirroring signals in their environment, children learn about their place within it. The CBI uses the physical circle to provide a contained environment; within the circle children mirror movements and vocalizations that are safety seeking and affiliative. The physical and conceptual circle is perhaps our most valuable tool for working with children.

The movement and music sequences for the beginning circle may vary with each group but adhere to a consistent formula: they are (1) simple, (2) repetitive, and (3) harmonious. If the physical circle provides containment, promoting safety, the activities within the circle must reinforce this safety. The goal of these activities and the formula they follow is to reshape the experience of the world following trauma, to rebuild the shattered assumptions: (1) "I am unworthy" (lowered self-esteem), (2) "The world is not dependable" (lack of trust), and (3) "It is my fault, and I am alone in this" (experience of isolation). The formula addresses these shattered assumptions in the following ways. (1) The experience of engaging in simple movement sequences that the children can master may increase their self-esteem. (2) The sequences use rhythm and music so that they are repetitive, creating ritual, which by definition is predictable. The rituals dependably return with each circle, encouraging the development of trust. (3) The experience of harmony reduces the sense of isolation. When a child moves to music, he experiences connection; when that same child moves to music and experiences peers mirroring that movement, affiliation is experienced; when vocalization accompanies the shared movement, integration may begin.

Psychoeducation

Because trauma is by nature overwhelming and because it causes children and adults to feel confused and out of control, giving individuals information about trauma can help them reestablish a sense of control and therefore recover more quickly. Psychoeducational interventions geared to students provide a developmentally sensitive cognitive map for understanding what makes frightening events traumatic to individual students, what normal reactions to these abnormal events are, and what is known about helping students recover.

This is a key concept to embrace when working with children and youth who have been exposed to difficult circumstances. Threat, terror, or traumatic exposures can be "felt about," but they can also be "thought about." It is important that facilitators are able to steward youth into safe experiences of thinking about their overwhelming experience (or traumatic exposures) so the child has more than one response to choose from when reexperiencing the original threat or danger.

Teaching kids to think about the concrete aspects of what has happened, absent the feeling state, allows an opportunity to practice appraisal and to engage in cognitive meaning making, hopefully in tandem with feeling states.

Art (silent stories)

A primary method, used over the last 150 years by therapists helping people exposed to overwhelming threat and violent events, has been "talk therapy." In fact, this process, "talking it out," is an accepted standard among many professionals in the human services field, for good reason. When something is truly bothering us, we can feel much better after we speak about it, after we get it off our chest. Recent neuroimaging evidence suggests this tactic may be ill advised for those significantly impacted by traumatic experiences. When trauma victims were asked to verbally express their trauma narrative while being scanned by MRI, results indicated that the auditory lexicon of the brain shut down as if "speechless" in the face of the terror.[1] Yet the visual lexicon of the brain appears able to process the trauma narrative, accessing and expressing visual symbols related to the traumatic experience without the same hesitation and blockage. Although these and similar findings give rise to numerous theories about what actually may be taking place in the brain physiology of trauma survivors, we do know that traumatic memory is not stored sequentially but rather in fragments, as if the experience is too horrifying to "take in" as a logical integrated sequence.

Verbal expression, or the tool of language, depends on logic and standard sequencing to make meaning of perception and experience. The CBI methodology assumes that horrifying experience is stored in the memory in nonsequential fragments and should not be processed, at least not in the beginning phases of intervention, using verbal techniques. Thus we use the idea of the "silent story," the use of visual representations of remembered experience to express, to bring from the inside to the outside, the traumatic narrative. A simple example of this, taken directly from the CBI intervention, asks youth to tell a silent story (we call it a story, rather than a drawing, because we want to generate the concept of narrative and we don't want youth to have performance anxiety around being a "good" artist) about what they thought was actually happening during the threat or traumatic event. This process results in profound expressions of the threat event without having to use words. A sequential narrative of the event is conducted on paper using visual imagery. Then the storytellers voluntarily speak about their picture (rather than the actual event) to the rest of the group. This appears to engender a safe, ordered, and meaningful expression of an otherwise unspeakable event.

The silent story method is used in the majority of the fifteen CBI sessions beginning with the silent story of safe place, and the silent story of strengths and fears, and ending with a collective silent story (a collective or group drawing done in silence) about building a village together. The traumatic images are transformed to curative images over the fifteen sessions. The verbal words used to describe these images during the fifteen sessions transform from hesitant and fragmented words to flowing and integrated sentences.

The silent stories are kept by the CBI participant, serving as a visual record of her traumatic narrative and as a visual navigation tool for her to note her story's transformation and piece together the story fragments into an integrated, meaningful whole.

Music

We do not require music for the CBI, but our experience shows that it may augment the positive effects of the CBI intervention. Music can shape the treatment and educational environment by soothing, empowering, grounding, and nurturing a sense of hope or safety. The group leader introducing and implementing exercises that evoke memories of traumatic events may precede these exercises with music that may soothe and calm both the participants and the group leader. Appropriate music may help the participants to feel less anxious and more resilient as they confront the painful material that the group exercises bring forth.

In addition, rhythmicity appears to be a universal phenomenon observed in all life forms, from the simplest to the most profound. It is evident in the ordered repetition of every human biological function (the beating of the heart, the cycle of inhalation and exhalation, and the contractions of the womb). A component of every human movement, rhythm is believed to be an attribute of central nervous system patterning.[2]

Rhythm and movement, it is hypothesized, have the capacity to organize individuals and groups, to promote healing, and to alter affect. The nonverbal exchanges offered in movement and music therapy are effective for traumatized children because body movements are children's natural means of expression and communication. Children can communicate, via movement, experiences for which there are no words. The use of consistent rhythmic movements can help the traumatized child to gain a sense of trust in the environment, which has betrayed her. The term *environment* may include the physical, social, and intrapsychic. Functionally, all aspects of behavior (physical, cognitive, and psychosocial) affect and influence each other.

The interrelationship of these various aspects of behavior when we are using rhythm and movement in treatment has positive implications. Not only might the participant gain a more positive sense of the world around him but he may also develop a more positive cognitive experience, translated as "hope." The importance of rhythm as a link to the earth and to others, and the recognition of the wisdom, which is both hidden and overt in the body, is focal in this work. With music and movement as catalysts, the child experiences the crucial importance of perceiving patterns and relationships, while striving for a balance between freedom and discipline.

Individuals' perceptions of symbol and of reality simultaneously work to enhance an integrated sense of self, with the self being experienced as a part of a greater reality. This greater reality can be experienced through the use of consistent, repetitive movement patterns as reliable and safe. To best support the children who have been betrayed by their experiences of terror and loss, treatment and psychosocial services should include movement and music intervention.

The movement and music intervention will rely heavily on music that is universally familiar and that can be an agent for easing depression and grief, soothing and relaxing, energizing, and enhancing the state of psychological joy, such as classical music and chants. The predominant beat to be used will support the rhythm, movement, and idea of the circle, of enclosure, of containment. This will normally be a ¼ or ⅚ rhythm. The group leader may also incorporate indigenous folk songs and other familiar children's music. Using such culturally familiar music as a teacher-child containment intervention can be a powerful element of CBI.

Cooperative games

Through the methodology of cooperative games, children and youth are offered a consistent structure and membership that promotes familiarity and security. Each group pursues high-energy cooperative games that are designed to bring joy and energy to the group, enhance communication among members, and create an environment of trust and empathy within the group. These cooperative games aim to capture children's attention and draw them into the group. Each activity offers a variety of ways to participate, and each child's level of participation is determined by her own level of comfort. Group leaders respect these choices, provided that they are not inimical to individual or group safety.

To be cooperative, games must meet three criteria. First, all the activities allow everyone to win. Simply participating and having fun ensures success. This should be made clear to each participant before each game, thus freeing children and youth from the pressures of having to perform and achieve. Second, the success of one child hinges on the success of all other children. Activities are designed so that success is achieved through group effort, requiring mutual support and cooperation. Participants become aware of the needs of others and gain practical experience in responding to those needs in order to achieve a shared goal. In turn they feel less isolated and develop a positive sense of themselves and their interpersonal effectiveness. As a result, feelings of empowerment, pride, and enhanced self-esteem emerge.

Third, physical successes are easily obtainable by all participants. By experiencing these successes, young people develop a sense of competency, mastery, and improved body image. They increasingly view themselves as sturdy, secure, and capable. We have found that the success of the cooperative games is partially dependent on the amount of safe physical space the group leader can provide for playing the game. Some of the cooperative games require more space than others. In each CBI training we identify the games that are most adaptable to limited spaces.

It is important for youth interventionists to understand that the CBI cooperative games are designed to foster cooperation, teamwork, and ultimately affiliation between group members involved in the cooperative game. If there is competitive behavior during the CBI cooperative game, then it is not a cooperative game, and its core objectives of increasing self-worth, self-esteem, and social perspective taking will fail. There is an unfortunate myth growing among some psychosocial interventionists that if you put violence-exposed youth into a sports program and let them have a good competitive experience their trauma will magically evaporate, and that it is "so much cheaper" than all those other "complicated interventions." This is a quick-fix mentality that should be avoided at all costs. CBI embraces the idea of game as the idea of cooperative problem solving in the service of adaptive coping. We do not consider *game* to have anything to do with winning but rather to have everything to do with affiliation, the opposite of isolation.

Drama games

Drama games are exercises aimed at practicing the elements necessary for recovery from trauma, that is, they counter the pervasive sense of powerlessness, psychic numbing, emotional dysregulation, isolation, and disconnection. They can be very useful in augmenting the natural recovery process following debriefing, especially with respect to building resiliency.

One of the common effects of exposure to traumatic events is a sense that one has only an external *locus of control*, meaning that the person feels powerless in his life, as if he has no internal control over the events taking place. So it appears to him that events simply happen and he has no ability to shape the events, relationships, or the future. Therefore there is no point in trying to plan for the future or to imagine another outcome; he may feel simply adrift and subject to the external currents.

The drama games focus on relocating the locus of control internally. We encourage children to be the directors of their fate, to use their imaginations to create and practice another outcome. They begin to develop their own internal dialogues to help them recognize, make sense of, and modulate their emotional responses to external events. This then allows them to experience their feelings without being overwhelmed by those feelings, to make sense of those feelings, and to continue to act with a sense of power and control.

Using the medium of drama allows children and youth to experience new learning on several levels at once. They practice putting words to their feelings, concretizing those feelings in a visual image and experiencing the new learning kinesthetically by moving through an action. In addition, many of these exercises are repeated so that each child has the opportunity of both watching the drama unfold and participating in it by taking several different roles. Acting "as if" gives a child role training and preparation for emotional expression in the moment. Increasing a child's repertoire of roles decreases emotional constriction, often an aftereffect of exposure to trauma. Further, drama game participants are using nonverbal language to share experiences, and this gives them the opportunity to retell their stories without accessing the auditory lexicon or cognitive processes disturbed by traumatic exposure.

Finally, the drama games are a group activity. They require a great deal of cooperation and interaction among group members. The children and youth are using the language of relationships to share experiences with one another and to counter the sense of isolation and disconnection that exposure to trauma often elicits. The drama games constantly focus children's attention on how they are related to other children and adults around them, on how they are connected to the world and how those connections may be influenced by their individual choices. The connections among group members are often physical as well as emotional, and each exercise is followed by a group processing time when group members can share with each other what the experience of going through the exercise felt like. The drama games may be very effective after traumatic exposure because they are fun to participate in, they use nonverbal expression, and they create a shared experience, drawing the group members closer together while also offering individuals the ability to control those connections.

Our intervention is designed to give the CBI group leader the time and supervision after each drama game exercise for all the participants to verbally share their impressions and thoughts about their participation in the drama game. This opportunity must always be offered to each participant before moving on. We have found this structure to be critically important in our work. We use drama games as simple games that allow peers in an ongoing group to warm up to each other and explore basic emotions and relationships in a safe and structured environment. Drama games are not intended to be and are never used as psychodrama.

Overarching principles of CBI

Throughout the course of the intervention, each session is guided by several overarching principles that are aimed at helping children heal or develop resiliency in critical ways.

Use rituals

Establishing rituals for the beginning, middle, and end of each group session brings a consistent, dependable component to an unpredictable future. Carried out in a group setting, these rituals reduce the child's sense of isolation. For example, encouraging children to "set up" and "put away" session materials in a rhythmic, repetitive manner—that is, as a regular ritual—may help them to gain (1) a sense of respect for their physical and social environments, (2) a sense of dependability, and (3) a sense of internal control over their environment that may support feelings of empowerment, mastery, and resiliency.

Make smooth transitions

Among traumatized children, fear escalates during transitions of any kind. As transitions take the child away from the present moment, which is known and secure, the unpredictability represents a threat to safety, groundedness, and stability and the child may interpret the loss of these essential connections as a threat to survival. Therefore, in moving from one activity or environment to another, smooth transitions that employ music, ritualized movement or games, and eye contact are essential.

Be consistent

Creating a treatment intervention environment in the classroom that is consistent, and features reliable cues encourages the development of trust between the children and between them and their leader(s). Repetition—for example, in the recurrence of anticipated events such as engaging in beginning and ending circle rituals and having same structure for each intervention—is most necessary and supports committed group participation.

Use open-ended directions and questions

To facilitate active engagement, exploration, and dialogue when addressing the topics introduced in each class, it is best to use *open-ended* directions such as, "Describe a time when you . . ." or open-ended questions such as, "What were you thinking when . . .?" or, "What was your reaction during . . .?" Using open-ended directions and questions allows traumatized youth to articulate their experiences in detailed and meaningful ways so they can build a story about the traumatic experience that makes sense to them. The use of questions that can be answered simply with yes or no is strongly discouraged.

Use themes

Each class is designed to address specific thematic content. The themes have psychoeducational, therapeutic, and metaphorical value. The associated creative and expressive activities and cooperative games suggested for each class provide a way for the students to actively engage with that thematic content.

Use some fantasy in cooperative games

The rules and required pieces of equipment for cooperative games provide a critical skeleton for each activity. When fantasy is added to this structure, basic games, which are simply a collection of rules, are transformed into fabulous adventures, capable of expanding the minds and experiences of all participants. For fantasy to be effective, we must ensure that the fantasies we use are developmentally appropriate, relevant to the group's goals, stimulating, and safe.

Most games consist of players trying to achieve an objective while observing various rules. For example, we might have a game in which the participants must simply collect objects and bring them back to a base without being tagged by the instructor. Once participants are tagged by the instructor, they must wait for a team member to tag them again, and then they can proceed with the game. By adding fantasy to this collection of basic rules, we can give this game a new "personality" to which each child can assign meaning. We can imagine, for example, that the children are "squirrels" and that the objects they are trying to obtain are "nuts." We can imagine that the instructor is a "fox" and that the base is in an underground squirrel home. We now have an enhanced game that we might call "Squirrels and Nuts." Through such added fantasies children and youth can play physically in the present while their minds indulge in an adventure outside their "real" or "normal" world. This allows youth to practice mastery in a world under their own control.

If this fantasy proves too frightening, we can change it to one that is less threatening to the group. By changing the fantasy but keeping the rules and objectives the same, we can make this and other games safe and stimulating for a wide range of developmental levels.

Allow choices

Traumatized youth certainly need to experience a sense of safety and control as they participate in the CBI. Giving traumatized youth too many choices can decrease their sense of safety and control. Yet, if the CBI progresses successfully, and especially with the older youth, it may be important to offer participants choices from a small menu of activities for the central activity or the cooperative game. Remember to exercise restraint in the number of choices presented and to offer activity selections that support the theme(s) of the particular session.

Work toward grounding and calming

The key word in working toward grounding and calming is *low*. One claims and transmits a grounded sense of physical closeness to the earth through literally reducing input to the senses, using a low voice, low lights, low body position. When children are experiencing chaos or lack of control in themselves or in the environment, any attempt to bring order and calmness to the group or to the child must never be communicated as competitive. Becoming bigger or brighter or louder to overwhelm chaos or disorder will only cause the child to attempt the same. Children who are running, screaming, or in any way avoiding becoming attentive to calm music will respond to the classroom leader who joins the music. This may be accomplished visually, kinesthetically, or auditorily. The leader may sit quietly in a prominent position and move gracefully to the music, may dim the lights in the room, or may whisper the lyrics to the music, softly, quietly. In this way the leader partners with the soothing rhythm of the music, enticing the children to join. Children who have lost control will appreciate and respond to these visual and auditory aids. Each action will produce the desired result of calming the children and giving back to them their sense of self-control (of the body, of the voice) as they choose to join rather than fight the leader and the rhythm of the music. Combining these approaches (sitting in a low posture; speaking in a soft, low voice; lowering the lights in the room from bright to dim) may make the reconnection more efficient.

Encourage being in the present tense

Living in the moment gives an individual, for that moment, the experience of being part of a greater reality, and of being connected with the continuum of life—the circle composed of past, present, and future, of life and death, of that which is infinite, yet knowable. In this moment there is no longing for the past or anxiety about the future; here is where all matter is transformed; this moment is so precious it will never be repeated. It must therefore be experienced completely, with no longing or anxiety. The use of *present tense* instructional words encourages children to be in the moment, with the music. For example, the leader might say, "Now we are sitting on the floor." These words tell the children what they are doing in the moment. Your speaking as you are doing gives the children and youth a more holistic experience of the moment; they simultaneously hear and act what they are doing. If the words are spoken rhythmically or sung to the music, the experience of the present is augmented.

Avoid sending conflicting messages

It is important to remember that children access new information visually; it is their most comfortable mode for receiving communication. Movement, consequently, is their most comfortable mode for expressive communication. Therefore the leader who is comfortable moving to a rhythm and can keep that response consistent will easily entice the children to join in that movement. The leader who can comfortably move his or her voice to that rhythm as well will draw the children into that rhythm more efficiently. This combination of gesture or movement and voice expressing a rhythm will give the children the experience of a more integrated sense of self and of the world around them. This combination is especially moving for children who are traumatized and for those who experience the world (and the self) as fragmented. However, a leader who is not comfortable moving his or her voice to an established rhythm should conduct in silence. When the gestural language expresses the rhythm, even in silence, the children will follow the rhythm. However, a leader whose voice expresses a rhythm different from the one his or her body and the music communicate will send conflicting messages. This will be at least confusing and at worst damaging to children who are already traumatized and experiencing themselves as fragmented.

The CBI has evolved over the last four years to integrate core methods of silent storytelling, music, movement and dance, cooperative games, and drama games for the explicit purpose of engendering expressive narrative about horrifying experience within a highly structured theme-based intensive psychosocial intervention. Following is the CBI session index for the fifteen-session classroom-based psychosocial intervention for youth survivors of trauma (ages five to eleven and twelve to eighteen):

Week one: Information, safety, and control

Class one	Information and safety: group rules ("how fear protects me") and making the "safe covers"
Class two	Information and control: review group rules ("what happens to me when I am afraid")
Class three	Safety and control ("my safe place")

Week two: Stabilization, awareness, and self-esteem

Class four	Stabilization and awareness ("where and how I feel fear and strength in my body")
Class five	Awareness ("this is what happens when I am mad, sad, and glad")
Class six	Self-esteem ("what I like to do and what I am good at")

Week three: Survival narrative—thoughts and reactions during danger to me and my loved ones

Class seven	Cognitive danger ("what I think was actually happening during the danger")
Class eight	Reaction narrative: emotional and physical ("reactions during the danger and what I felt in my body")
Class nine	Integration narrative: cognitive-emotional-physical integration ("after the danger passed")

Week four: Survival narrative—resource identification and coping skills

Class ten	Appraisal narrative: resource identification ("what I have lost and what has changed")
Class eleven	Appraisal narrative: coping skills ("helping during the danger")
Class twelve	Appraisal narrative: coping skills ("what I feel right now: safety and strength")

Week five: Resource installation and future planning

Class thirteen	Social narrative: salutogenic prompts ("learning new things about myself")

Class fourteen   Social narrative: connection with significant oth-
                 ers ("friends and trust")
Class fifteen   Social narrative: future orientations ("let's build a
                 village together")

Notes

1. Orr, S. P. (June 21, 1997). Psychophysiologic reactivity to trauma-related imagery in PTSD: Diagnostic and theoretical implications of recent findings. *Annals of the New York Academy of Science, 821,* 114–124.
2. Berrol, C. F. (1992). The neurophysiologic basis of the mind/body connection in dance therapy. *American Journal of Dance Therapy, 14*(1).

ROBERT D. MACY *is executive director, the Center for Trauma Psychology; codirector, National Center for Child Traumatic Stress Network-Category III; and director, Community Services, the Trauma Center-Boston. In collaboration with codirector Bessel van der Kolk, he is responsible for the Category III design, development, and service delivery management of the national initiative to research and treat child and adolescent posttraumatic stress disorders funded by the Substance Abuse and Mental Health Services Administration. Macy is also the director of psychosocial initiatives at the Trauma Center-Boston and founder of the Community Services Program, which manages the Metro Boston Trauma Response Network for Youth.*

DICKI JOHNSON MACY *is the creative director for the Center for Trauma Psychology, the director of Center Studio, and the codirector of Project Joy, a nonprofit foundation dedicated to providing group-based psychotherapeutic services to homeless toddlers and youth.*

STEVEN I. GROSS *is the program director for the Center for Trauma Psychology, the director of community services, a program of the psychosocial initiatives at the Trauma Center-Boston, and the codirector of Project Joy.*

PAMELA BRIGHTON *is the development director for the Center for Trauma Psychology and the clinical director of the Penikese Island School.*

The specific case of Eastern Germany is illustrative of a more general framework for how identity formation, family processes, and humiliation, alienation, and deprivation are linked to local conditions or situational contexts.

4

A culture of threat: Right-wing extremism and negative identity formation in German youth

Wolfgang Edelstein

A NEW EXTREMISM in German youth has emerged in the years since Germany's reunification, in the former East Germany much more intensively than in the former West Germany. However, the main components of right-wing extremism—xenophobia and nationalism, anti-Semitism, and ideological commitment to authoritarianism, inequality, and racism—do not constitute an indissoluble conceptual unity. Xenophobia is the lead variable. According to surveys, it affects at least one-third of the youth population, and considerably more among those who fall within the lower social economic strata. According to the recent IEA (International Association for the Evaluation of Educational Achievement) Civics Study,[1] fifteen-year-old Germans held the most xenophobic attitudes across the twenty-eight participating countries. Anti-Semitism is on the rise, though perhaps rather less so than in other European countries, and the reasons behind that anti-Semitism

NEW DIRECTIONS FOR YOUTH DEVELOPMENT, NO. 98, SUMMER 2003 © WILEY PERIODICALS, INC.

appear to be generated less from within than as a partial consequence of the Israeli-Arab conflict.

Every study shows that in Eastern Germany (the former German Democratic Republic, or GDR) the incidence of extremism, as measured by various indicators, is about twice as frequent as in the West. More than 50 percent of all racist, xenophobic, and neo-Nazi incidents, and especially of all such *violent* incidents, have happened in the Eastern provinces, where less than 20 percent of the German population lives. In this sense, Eastern Germany appears more similar to Eastern Europe than to Western Germany. In Eastern Europe a neo-Nazi youth movement is definitely a threat.

I look at this reality as less a German problem than as a general problem that emerges in Germany under specific conditions. In this chapter I want to look at the problem with a view to the condition of youth in the modern world more generally. Treatment of the local problem should be seen as vicarious, although the phenomenology of brutality and violence, the symbolic presentations of the self, the cultural manifestations and the historical associations certainly vary across cultures and territories. Universal features of adolescent risk factors are involved together with regional or local ones. I shall try to specify some conditions for the rise of an extremist youth culture, as an example of a structure of risk that affects a generation involved in social, economic, and sociocultural transition.

Who becomes a Nazi?

Normatively, right-wing extremism represents moral waywardness in thinking and in action. The concept of moral deprivation or waywardness points to the psychosocial and moral implications of a syndrome that combines economic, familial, educational, and cultural factors in variable ways. The causal relationships are not as clear, but the correlates of social dispossession and the dissolution of institutional bonds are clear. Adolescents may respond to these realities with hedonism or rebellion, far too often with moral indifference. Adolescents who are failure prone in apprenticeships following unsuccessful school careers, who wind up being unsuccessful in jobs, may respond with ideologically violent or socially rebellious reactions that protect their self-esteem. Such responses may be viciously extremist, xenophobic, racist, and anti-Semitic and may be in deep contrast to the moral conventions that until very recently have been more or less unanimously accepted as the basis of social action in the Federal Republic of Germany.

It is their refusal to heed these conventions, generally accepted since the downfall of the Third Reich in 1945, that turns the youthful rebels into racists and neo-Nazis. Needless to say, trying to comprehend the motives for this development does not imply that we are accepting the rebels' nazi convictions or justifying their stance out of compassion for the underdog or a position of solidarity with an emerging underclass. But we need to ask questions about the origins of this development, and while opposing their actions and beliefs, we need to view these youth as victims of their economic, social, and psychological condition. Paraphrasing the title of one of Anna Seghers's stories,[2] the question is, How does a man become a Nazi? Who becomes a Nazi? What kind of person is receptive to Nazi values? What are the conditions and contexts that turn people into Nazis? And finally, are there ways and means to counteract such developments?

Anna Seghers reconstructs the socialization of Fritz Müller in humiliated post-Versailles Germany, where soldiers return home, unemployed and devastated, to bring up their children in misery. These children of *losers* in their families, schools, and peer groups develop corresponding mechanisms of compensation, character traits, and motives of spite and revenge that take them, first, into the ranks of the storm trooper thugs, later into the SS, and finally, during the war in Eastern Europe, to their well-known involvements in concentration camps, firing squads, and mass murder in Polish and Russian villages and ghettos (as described by Christopher Browning,[3] ordinary men). Fritz's brothers join the youth movement or the Communist Party, and Fritz joins the Nazis.

Seghers describes the collective impoverishment in which Fritz's individual family is placed as well as the solidarity of the deprived. In this setting Fritz and his likes can earn recognition and praise from the Nazis by transcending the boundaries to violence and exerting power in the form of terror. Fritz finds himself master of life and death. This occurs rather by happenstance in the early years, but later, in Russia, he is systematic and goal oriented, entirely intentional. There is, indeed, much to remind one of Palestinian suicide bombers but also certainly much that is different. Both the similarities and the differences are important and should concern us.

All individuals have potential for development, but psychosocial needs and social opportunities determine how individuals use their potential: whether they use it for social adjustment or for a career as moral exemplars or whether they become maladapted neurotics or outright monsters. Beyond the social structures that operate behind individuals' backs, differential opportunity structures decide their fortunes. Among these differential factors we note social class and family, schools and teachers, and peer groups; all provide differential reinforcement for needs and dispositions.

The role of school

Seghers draws a picture of Fritz Müller's school experience. Different teachers exert different influences by using contrasting modalities of shaping and modeling with their dependent pupils. There is a liberal and progressive teacher who overtaxes Fritz with his good intentions, leading to the unintended consequence of moving him closer to his destiny. There is a Nazi teacher who recognizes Fritz's restricted potential but instrumentalizes it and promotes his successful monster's career. Seghers sensitively reconstructs the psychology of first the young then the adolescent schoolboy; his psychology could have opened a pathway to a conventional conduct of life, but it also had the potential to open the gate toward a different type of career, a different kind of normalcy.

Recognition and humiliation are central dimensions of adolescent experience, especially in school. Recognition and humiliation are woven into the fabric of pedagogy and instruction. They are aspects of teachers' and students' roles, inevitable aspects of instruction, part of grades and feedback, tests and exercises. What is the involuntary part of school in development, and what is the voluntary influence exerted through grades and the evaluation culture of the school? School plays an essential role in the emergence of the extreme right, as we may derive from individual stories such as Seghers's account of Fritz Müller's career from deprived childhood to Nazi killer.

More to the point, perhaps, are recent data from youth surveys like Dietmar Sturzbecher's about youth and violence in Eastern Germany.[4] These surveys demonstrate that large numbers of disaffected adolescents are disappointed with school and see very little meaning in the subjects they are taught. They are lost and distraught in their schools and distrust their teachers, holding them accountable for their boredom, seeing them as completely disinterested in students' lives and fortunes, and accusing them of a humiliating aloofness from students' problems. Up to 40 percent of students in comprehensive schools and vocational secondary schools in Brandenburg voice these complaints. It is this very group of the educationally underprivileged who are the breeding ground of right-wing extremism.

The school experience of young people is of interest, not so much because the responsibility for the emergence of extreme right-wing positions in youth should be attributed to the school, but because we ought to give the role of the school in the development of *educational failure* more hard thought, together with the role that schools might play in the *prevention* of such developments. How could the school shape school experience to prevent losers from seeking an extremist compensation for their failure? How could a culture of the school provide its youthful members with a world of experiences that generates immunity from neo-Nazi or other right-wing temptations and impulses to extremist action? What can the school do to effectively oppose the active components of the extremist syndrome: xenophobia, anti-Semitism, a racist affirmation of inequality, and excessive nationalism? What are the cognitive and affective strategies, the designs of instruction, the modalities of shaping the classroom and school climates that counteract the assimilation of adolescents into extremist subcultures? To come up with viable answers to these questions, we need to understand the real causes of right-wing extremism among young people.

Causes and antecedents

Certain changes in the macro-system have psychosocial consequences. These changes produce contexts of experience that interact with the developmental vulnerabilities of adolescents (mostly adolescents in quest of identity), who, given specific contingencies in the actual social context, tend to develop dispositions toward extremist orientations. Among the macro-system elements that are independent factors in this analysis, the two most important are anomie and individualistic modernization. Anomie and individualistic modernization represent psychosocial consequences of *long processes* of social transformation. On the micro-level a third, more limited factor is the kind of authoritarian personality syndrome seen to grow out of dismissive attachment patterns in childhood. Although this syndrome can arise in any social context and presumably at any historical time, it may emerge with greater saliency due in particular cohorts. It is cohort effects that effectively trigger the emergence of new orientations in youth and thus call for a detailed analysis of their psychological effects on individual and social development. Glen Elder's description of the children of the Great Depression is one model of this type of analysis.[5] An analogy may be the children of German unification.

At the end of the nineteenth century Émile Durkheim introduced the notion of *anomie* to describe the social and moral consequences of the breakdown that was occurring in traditional society with its stable social formations, rules, and value systems. This breakdown marked the transition to modern society characterized by the industrial division of labor. Traditional society had been organized through intergenerationally stable rules of "mechanical solidarity," with little room for individual variation and for individual influence on the social order. Whereas traditional loyalties and duties had once persisted against the onslaught of *individual needs, goals, and desires,* the latter came to be decisive influences in the market-dominated world of competitive capitalism that succeeded the traditional world of personal bonds, inherited skills, and natural exchange. In the wake of the transition, *individual* achievement and *individual* judgment had to provide a foundation for the new and more flexible moral order of "organic solidarity."

But the bleak side of this development into a higher-order organization is fragmentation and disorganization. When the social potentials that sustain the division of labor and the functionally required responsibility of individuals are disorganized, contradictory, and antagonistic, when people are unable to reconstitute social life in terms of a subjectively meaningful sociomoral order, then social and cognitive conflicts bring about structural and psychological disorder. This involves a loss of moral consistency that leads to an anomic withdrawal of the person, whose motivation now depends primarily on his or her own needs and desires. Durkheim diagnosed anomie as a condition of socially generated individual risk, as a deprivation of the socially sustained meaning of life, and as a retreat from action. (In the extreme case this brings about depression and even death, in the case of anomic suicide.) Logically, however, alienation and deprivation of meaning in disorganized social structures may be met with equal effectiveness not by depressive withdrawal but by the contrary strategy of rebellious action: by rejecting the accepted public moral coordinates of action, by refusing control and turning against the prevailing norms and expectations in antimoral rebellion.

Durkheim interpreted the consequences of the transition from traditional society to the industrial order in terms of the gains made by members of society in individual autonomy and autonomous moral regulation, and he described the negative consequences and correlates of the transition in terms of a failure or inability to practice this autonomy. A century later his perspective has again become relevant. But now the transition is from the established and consolidated forms of capitalism to new global forms of capitalist production, marketing, and finance. In global market competition, winners once again gain autonomy and competence, and losers remain paralyzed in the forced inaction of unemployment and often of alienation and depression as well. The specific deprivation of meaning suffered by the losers in the present transition is loss of meaning of the subjective individual future, that is, the loss of a constructive and motivated orientation toward the future. As a consequence, anomie emerges on both the individual and the collective levels and on both the local and the global plane. The available alternative is an aggressively antisocial, anomic rebellion.

To bring the Durkheimian analysis of anomie to bear on the local and cohort-specific phenomena that are relevant to the extremist youth rebellion in Eastern Germany, it must be applied to that region's sudden transition from the rigidly stable and centrally planned organization of the GDR to Western-style capitalism in the year 1989. The transition generated a sudden destabilization of individual lives among the parents of those who were ten- to twenty-year-olds at the time. It disrupted the expectancies and normative orientations of many people, and was followed, in the more vulnerable young cohorts, by a loss of trust in the new social order, its institutions, and its representatives. All support for organized youth activities ceased at that moment. Institutions for adolescent training and leisure—formerly supports of the socialist state and of socialist education—were discontinued (and no substitutes provided), and a great number of adolescents were left deprived of action opportunities, organization, and perspective. The disempowerment of the former elites coincided with widespread unemployment in the parent generation, especially among the former elites (state employees, teachers, and politically active or merely loyal groups), a humiliation perceived and processed by the young. The deindustrialization of the infrastructure took place together with the discontinuation of public institutions designed to channel the activities of youth. The result was widespread disaffection in the young generation. Surveys showed (and continue to show) distrust concerning both the present and the future with regard to the economy and the integrity of life perspectives. Many young people were suddenly deprived of per-spectives, orientations, and expectations, and exposed to the experience of cohort-specific deprivation. In that cohort (youth between the ages of thirteen or fourteen and twenty-five), some individuals reacted with violence. This violence was directed most of all against foreigners, especially dark-skinned asylum seekers, but also against even handicapped or homeless persons as the putative, real or symbolic, beneficiaries of the new welfare system, which was believed to redistribute this cohort's entitlements to "social parasites" and to deprive the Germans of their rightful heritages. But probably these youth were reacting mostly to their own humiliation and designing a loser's revenge on those who they believed were underserved winners. They could turn their backs on the unsatisfactory present and look, for the preservation of pride, to a better (imaginary) past, which due to the failure of socialism had to be a past before socialism. Thus they came to wear the insignia of racial superiority and to use their bullying power to redeem themselves from the status of victims of an uncomprehended development. Vindicating their empowerment through appropriation of a putatively glorious past, an empowerment validated by the use of brute force against whoever opposes them, apparently compensates for what is subliminally felt to be the expropriation and dispossession of a failed generation.

Risk and social transformation

Let me turn now from the development of anomie in the unification cohort to the collateral *long process* of institutional transformation. Ulrich Beck and Anthony Giddens[6] have called this process the *second,* or *reflexive,* modernization. Using a concept that has gained wide currency, Beck speaks about the emergence of a *risk society,* because the new social order is characterized by weak social organizations that face difficulties and generate problems (*risks*) that can be traced to an increasing deinstitutionalization of social conduct and of the life course. Wilhelm Heitmeyer, of the University of Bielefeld,[7] has analyzed this process in terms of the diminishing stability of the institutions that channel and support the course of individual lives, especially the institution of the family. This *corrosion of ligatures* (to borrow Dahrendorf's term[8]) is represented by the gradual loss of the power of social institutions, such as the family, to regulate individual behavior and individual goals and intentions. This process is the outflow of the sustained, continuous rise of individualism: weak institutions throw open a *danger zone* through which the rising generations must travel, while the traditional agents of socialization progressively lose their power of direction and guidance, confronted by an increasing risk of loss of moral purpose. Traditions are corroded and diluted in the process, losing their function as *syntactic rules* for the collective conduct of individual lives. The reciprocal bonds of families weaken under the strain of market-driven interests. The weakness of family systems results in increasing frequencies of divorce, diminishing birthrates, and growing numbers of singles, all indicators of new, subinstitutional forms of life. The increasing length of formal education delays the beginning of economic independence and the formation of stable identities among the young, ironically increasing their dependence on the already weakened system. Thus there is increasing tension between the principle of personal attachment in families and the principle of competition in the school and on the market, a ubiquitous competition in achievements and lifestyles, jobs, and leisure activities.

The stress emanating from these tensions must be borne by the *individuals themselves*, as the weak institutions are no longer able to provide the normative support that people need psychologically. Thus economic modernization and intensified competition put people under increasing pressure from the forces of individualism. For those who experience losses in this process, the nostalgia of strong institutions, the flight into the security and relief of group power, and finally the abdication from individual moral standards and individual conscience represent a persistent temptation—sometimes critically identified as the lure of the fun society. In sum, individualization theory joins forces with anomie theory to spell out the consequences for the losers in the long processes of social and sociopsychological transformation.

Patterns of attachment

The theory of individualistic modernization is focused on the family as a weak institution framing strongly motivated individuals. Following Freud, Adorno's once-famous theory of the authoritarian personality explained that personality's genesis in terms of family dynamics.[9] The centerpiece of the theory is the concept of sons' idealization of, particularly, fathers, whose repression of the sons simultaneously produces authoritarian submission (to the strong father) and authoritarian aggression (against weak others). In a version of the theory expressly brought to bear on the family dynamics of neoauthoritarian individuals, the Freudian drive theory has been supplanted by John Bowlby's much more transparent attachment theory[10] as the basis of character formation. The types of *insecure attachment* specified by Bowlby (anxious, ambivalent, disorganized) have been complemented by a new type: the indifferent-dismissive or hostile type of insecure attachment. The dismissively attached switch off their feelings for their parents, drain the experiences with parents of their energy, and repress memories of pain, conflict, or humiliation, devaluing both the experience and the persons involved. Denial and devaluation are generalized to objects of negative cathexis, providing the humiliated subjects with an ample supply of victims and opportunities to project their feelings of hate and aggression and to compensate for their experience of shaming and devaluation.

This family fate can probably emerge in any society that encompasses a family dynamic as we know it. The attachment-based version, however, is more open to historical opportunity structures and their vicissitudes, which affect the attachment patterns of families in the context of societal development such as rapid political or economic change. The authors of the new attachment-based theory of the authoritarian personality, Christel Hopf and her associates,[11] have empirical support for the contention that in the GDR, the role of institutions in childhood did indeed affect the attachment patterns of families or family substitutes such that dismissive attachment appeared to youth to be a more or less viable strategy for avoiding and countering a system of continuous humiliation. And that experience calls for a revenge, which the authoritarian character is eager to supply.

Identity formation

We are indebted to Erik H. Erikson[12] for his classic theory of identity formation in the context of historical change. According to Erikson, ego identity is the feeling of trust in the reliable unity and continuity of the self, mirrored by supportive others. This is a feeling that provides strength and motivation for action in the present and hope and perspective for action in the future.

The construction of a viable identity generally requires successful resolution of the major conflicts that have dominated earlier phases of childhood. Successful resolution of these conflicts is followed by integration of the strengths and gains achieved in earlier phases of development with the help of supportive structures in families, preschools, and schools. Adolescence is a vulnerable phase in the life cycle and particularly dependent on the social forces, structures, and institutions in which it is embedded. Erikson has shown how a destructive family dynamic, for example an authoritarian and repressive relationship between father and son, may threaten the process of identity formation and put the son at risk of identity diffusion or disintegration, or identification with the aggressor.[13] Erikson places the individual case expressly in the context of historical change, using a case approach to bring the psychodynamic origins of a son's (antiauthoritarian) rebellion into the sociohistorical perspective.

Adolescence sets the stage for the development of a personal identity and for a person's integration into groups that provide strength to the ego, and it plays a decisive role in the development of a person's ideological perspective on self and society. Thus adolescent development is largely influenced by the social context in which a person is immersed. Beyond the family system and classroom peers, beyond social groups and political organizations, ideological movements and sociohistorical formations increasingly claim a right of place in adolescence. More than before, then, a person's process of identity formation is affected, and sometimes torn, by the vectors that dominate the macro-system–micro-system interface.

Collective identity

Erikson's *Life History and the Historical Moment* includes his essay on the process of *collective identity formation* among the protest generation of the 1960s and 1970s. This process is defined as "a critical phase marked by the *reciprocal aggravation of internal conflict and of societal disorganization*"[14] (emphasis mine), a definition that highlights the quality of macro-micro interaction. Erikson describes the changed economic, social, and cultural context of the new generation, its intellectual and experiential ecology, the conditions of a new historical consciousness, and a youthful awareness colored by the cognitive egocentrism that is constitutive of adolescent ideological thought. He labels the adolescent mode of thinking as the "all or nothing *totalistic* quality of adolescence, which permits many young people to invest their loyalty in simplistically over-defined ideologies"[15] (emphasis in the original). "The dominant issue for identity formation", Erikson wrote, is that "the selective ego is in charge and enabled to be in charge by a social structure which grants a given age group the place it needs, and in which it is needed."[16] What happens, we may ask, when the social situation subverts this vital condition?

Negative identity

The humanistic protest movement of the sixties pursued progressive goals of liberation and social justice. But the terms of identity formation theory are not constrained to serve the analysis of *positive* group identity. An important part of Erikson's work was

devoted to the clarification of identity diffusion—the psychodynamic, developmental, and social conditions that prevent, impair,
or delay the positive resolution of inner conflicts that is conducive
to a healthy or equilibrated identity. Unresolved conflicts con-
tribute to the pathography of adolescent failure to develop a stable
identity, generating some variety of identity diffusion instead: negative reciprocity, based in early mistrust; guilt and weakness; anger;
work paralysis; or depression.

Such symptoms frequently lead to the choice of a *negative identity*. The adolescent replaces the image of a weak and ambivalent
parent with a cruel and basically desperate self, a threatening exposure to a significant other's exercise of will with an excess of obedi-
ence and deference to leadership. He replaces the pressure for
activity with passive submission, and taxing expectations of
achievement with indolence or with offensive acts and norm violations. Transferring these events from the private to the public
space, replacing normal sociability with exclusion and with affiliation with criminal gangs, absorption into authoritarian group structures, or the adoption of racist ideologies, may provide a negative
substitute for an integrated identity.

The question then arises whether "a critical phase marked by *a
reciprocal aggravation of internal conflict and of societal organization*"
can be identified that provides an opportunity for an antiprogres-
sive, right-wing movement of youthful rebels to emerge in parts of
German society beset by specific sociohistorical vulnerabilities. I
refer of course to East Germany after the downfall of socialism and
unification (1989).

Rise of a culture of negative group identity

Earlier in this chapter I gave a rough description of the social context of adolescent experience following the downfall of the GDR.
That context did not provide an assurance that an active ego was
given the place it needed nor did it signal that it was indeed needed
at all. We understand that a situation of humiliation witnessed or
experienced, of opportunities unattained or foregone, of perspectives dimmed or reserved for others arouses anger and resentment

among those most affected by or sensitive to the threat of fore-
closure of their future. Whereas the corresponding affect is often
turned against those who, according to the terrible simplifications
of the populists, harvest the benefits from the allegedly unfair and
biased distribution of welfare (for example, to refugees, Jews, and
the handicapped), a positive cathexis rebelliously targets the Nazis,
whom both the past socialist regime and the present capitalist society identify as objects of moral and political shame and collective
guilt. The rebels refuse to share the public denial that is the essence
of civil consensus about Germany's Nazi past. Thus what has been
rejected and forbidden returns as the object of identification. There
is an emotionally charged concept of the nation and a chauvinistic
national sentiment that turns against the foreigners who allegedly
exploit the nation and appropriate for themselves the job opportunities illegitimately withheld from those who rightfully own them
and turns toward the Nazis, who according to the shared mythol-
ogy restored pride of place to a dispossessed German people. Neo-
Nazi identification, anti-Semitism, and xenophobia have therefore
become the hallmark of the ideology of a group of dispossessed and
disaffected young East Germans who draw strength, if not comfort, from a posture of rebellion and nonalignment with the majority culture (and also the hallmark of individuals who, less afflicted,
aspire to ideological or political leadership of such groups).

This recalls what happened with *contrary* intentions with the pro-
testers of the 1970s, and if we may believe the testimony of Anna
Seghers, the fascist youth of the 1920s. (Perhaps this is what moti-
vates, again with a different justification, the suicide squads of the
Palestinian Jihadis and anti-American young Arab terrorists.) What
seems to be common to them all is a vengeful attempt to obtain
control over their own lives and give them meaning after an experience of weakness, humiliation, and *loss of control*.[17] This is, after
all, the basic developmental function of the formation of identity
in youth. It is—a process failed at the cost of confusion, and sometimes depression and death, a process sometimes won at the cost of
one's life. This is the case in Germany, and other things being
equal, this is probably the case around the world.

Conclusion

While working on this paper it has gradually dawned on me that what I have tried to grasp may be less the special case of Eastern Germany than a much more general case. In my view, we are confronted worldwide with an emerging youth problem. Demographically, there have never been more adolescents in the world, and never as many youth exposed to processes of modernization, individualization, and the corrosion of tradition. Structurally, this is the situation in which anomie emerges.

In sum, we are confronted with the effects of the long historical processes of modernization and concomitant individualization worldwide. We don't think enough about the social psychological implications and potential political consequences of these processes, which are fraught with frustrations and humiliations. We tend to underestimate the developmental hazards affecting identity formation in a regime of increasing individualization and anomie. Contexts may vary from site to site around the world and strategies of protest and rebellion may differ from one local culture to the next. At the same time, youth are being exposed to a more or less unified media culture that aggravates the frustration and humiliation of the have-nots while feeding them on violence. In addition, we do not know what the experience of schooling is doing to the myriad adolescent minds thus prepared.

Notes

1. Torney-Purta, J., Lehmann, R., Oswald, H., & Schulz, W. (2001). *Citizenship and education in twenty-eight countries: Civic knowledge and engagement at age fourteen.* Amsterdam: International Association for the Evaluation of Educational Achievement.

2. Seghers, A. (1977). Becoming a Nazi. In *Collected works in single issues, Vol. IX: Stories 1926–1944* (pp. 285–298). Berlin: Aufbau Verlag.

3. Browning, C. R. (2001). *Ordinary men: Reserve Police Battalion 101 and the final solution in Poland.* London: Penguin.

4. Sturzbecher, D. (Ed.). (1997). *Youth and violence in East Germany.* Göttingen: Hogrefe; Sturzbecher, D. (2001). *Youth in East Germany: Lifeworld and delinquency.* Opladen: Leske & Budrich.

5. Elder, G. (1974). *Children of the great depression.* Chicago: University of Chicago Press.

6. Giddens, A. (1991). *Modernity and self-identity: Self and society in the late modern age.* Stanford, CA: Stanford University Press; Beck, U. (1992). *Risk society: Towards a new modernity.* London: Sage.

7. Heitmeyer, W., et al. (1995). *Violence: Negative aspects of individualization among adolescents from different environments.* Weinheim: Juventa.

8. Dahrendorf, R. (1994). Corrosion of ligatures and the utopia of cosmopolitanism. In U. Beck (Ed.), *Risky freedom: Individualization in modern societies* (pp. 421–436). Frankfurt/Main: Suhrkamp.

9. Adorno, T. W., Frenkel-Brunswik, E., Levinson, D. J., Sanford, R. N., et al. (1950). *The authoritarian personality.* New York: Harper & Row.

10. Bowlby, J. (1969). *Attachment and loss, Vol. 1: Attachment.* New York: Basic Books.

11. Hopf, C., Rieker, P., Sanden-Marcus, M., & Schmidt, C. (1995). *Family and right-wing extremism: Socialization processes and extremist orientations among young males.* Weinheim: Juventa.

12. Erikson, E. H. (1959). *Identity and the life cycle.* New York: International Universities Press. In *Psychological Issues, 1*(1); Erikson, E. H. (1975). *Life history and the historical moment.* New York: Norton; Erikson, E. H. (1968). *Identity, youth, and crisis.* New York: Norton.

13. Erikson (1959), chap. 1.

14. Erikson (1975), p. 195.

15. Erikson (1975), p. 204.

16. Erikson (1968), p. 246.

17. Skinner, E. A. (1996). A guide to constructs of control. *Journal of Personality and Social Psychology, 71,* 549–570; Frey, D. (2002). *Theoretical framework for the causes of the Nazi movement: A theory of cognitive control.* Unpublished paper, University of Munich.

WOLFGANG EDELSTEIN *is professor and director emeritus of the Max Planck Institute for Human Development, Berlin.*

When Bosnia-Herzegovina was thrown into war in the summer of 1991, one and a half million people lost their homes and were in flight. It was clear from the beginning that the extent of trauma would be enormous and evident for generations to come.

5

Capacity building in trauma therapy and trauma research in Bosnia-Herzegovina

Gisela Röper, Maria Gavranidou

WHEN BOSNIA-HERZEGOVINA was thrown into war in the summer of 1991, the whole of Europe and the United States of America were shocked about the cruelty with which this war was pursued. The historian Timothy Garton Ash[1] reported that 250,000 people were killed in the years between 1992 and 1995, most of them civilians. One and a half million people lost their homes and were in flight. About one million people were in camps, where systematic raping of women with the goal of impregnating them with the enemy's offspring was introduced as an element of warfare. It was clear from the beginning that the extent of traumatization would be enormous and evident for years, presumably for generations to come.

Bosnian health authorities in collaboration with international organizations were very aware that professional help was needed to support children in particular but also entire families who were traumatized and under the influence of ongoing threat. However,

NEW DIRECTIONS FOR YOUTH DEVELOPMENT, NO. 98, SUMMER 2003 © WILEY PERIODICALS, INC.

neither psychotherapists nor trauma specialists were available in the country. In the former Yugoslavia only the three largest universities—Belgrade, Zagreb, and Ljubljana—had a psychology faculty and offered courses in clinical psychology; no university in Bosnia-Herzegovina did so. The University of Sarajevo had offered only a course in educational psychology, a degree that prepared students to work as school psychologists.

Therefore professionals, whose training was somehow related to clinical psychology had to be recruited; among these recruits were professors of general psychology, the previously mentioned educational psychologists, teachers, medical personnel, and paraprofessionals who had been involved in social work with children and adolescents. Most of those helpers had been traumatized themselves and were highly concerned about the lack of specific knowledge and skills in both diagnostics and the treatment of trauma. Numerous foreign organizations as well as individual experts had already offered workshops in trauma therapy during the war, often in Croatia, near the border with Bosnia-Herzegovina. This tended to result in patchwork training, and the trainees had no help with integrating the various pieces of information and no case supervision. One exception was a systematic training course offered by the University of Munich, under the leadership of W. Butollo,[2] and a subsequent supervision course, by Butollo and Röper.

This specialization in trauma therapy course included a series of training workshops teaching theory and intervention for posttraumatic stress disorder (PTSD). For the trainers particularly, the supervision workshops were both challenging and gratifying. They were challenging because of all the horrifying stories of war trauma and gratifying because one could see the training content so skillfully applied by the trainees.

Between the end of the training and the beginning of the supervision course many of the course participants had already become supervisors in their regions, as they were usually the most qualified workers on their teams. Therefore the goal of this supervision course was to provide supervision and teach supervisor skills at the same time. General principles of supervision such as establishing the effects of the therapeutic work so far, pointing out specific personal skills of the therapist, and clarifying the next steps in therapy as well as an overall goal were, especially in the first two aspects mentioned, an entirely new form of supervision. Being praised instead of criticized by the trainer was a new and welcome experience of supervision for the participants. The positive working atmosphere in which the indeed impressively skilled and strongly motivated therapeutic work of the participants was discussed created a beautiful balance to the serious content of the workshops.

Initiating programs in Bosnia-Herzegovina

It was clear that this group of trained trauma specialists could be seen only as the beginning of providing professional mental health care in the country. Clinical psychology would have to be established in universities in Bosnia-Herzegovina to ensure that trained psychotherapists would be available in the future. A cooperative effort between the Department for Clinical Psychology (headed by W. Butollo) at the University of Munich and one university in each entity (the Federation Bosnia-Herzegovina and the Republic of Srpska) of Bosnia-Herzegovina was planned and an agreement was signed in 1999. Clinical psychology was to be established at the Universities of Sarajevo and Banja Luka. Banja Luka received support also from Belgrade University, therefore the support from Munich was considerably less for Banja Luka than for Sarajevo.

A curriculum was established for a one-year course in clinical psychology, which was to be the focus of the fourth and last year of study leading up to the diploma in psychology. Teaching was conducted by the visiting professors and additional colleagues from Munich, W. Butollo, G. Röper, and M. Gavranidou. Regular seminars were held by the two local assistants, E. Durakovic-Belko and S. Powell. Visiting professors from other countries, in particular the United States and Croatia, filled out the course. Teaching topics addressed the common major areas in clinical psychology. The teaching style differed somewhat from what the students in Sarajevo were used to because it was more interactive.

In addition, a completely new style of program was established, a practical program with the title Basic Skills in Psychotherapy. This program had been part of the Munich curriculum for nearly twenty years, and it was adapted to the conditions at the Universities of Sarajevo and Banja Luka. The classes were conducted by G. Röper in Sarajevo and U. Goldmann in Banja Luka. For the Sarajevo program, Röper taught twelve units together with the local assistants and also three young colleagues who were working in hospitals or international organizations in Sarajevo. The goal of this program was not only to teach a particular group of students but to involve the group of young colleagues in a way that would allow them to continue teaching this program in the future. Therefore each teaching unit was prepared in a workshop with the assistants; the workshops included theory and practice and concluded with discussion and feedback.

The Basic Skills in Psychotherapy program deals with basic intervention steps derived from cognitive behavior and gestalt therapies.[3] Students work in small groups role-playing the parts of client, therapist, and observer. The "therapist" follows the principles of one step of intervention, which has been presented in theory by one of the trainers and shown in a short demonstration. The trainers go around to the small groups to provide direct supervision. Each practice session is followed by a large-group discussion in which speakers for each small group share from their work and ask questions. These after-practice discussions prove extremely fruitful. This program has been highly appreciated by the students of Sarajevo and Banja Luka, seminars have been characterized by an atmosphere of high concentration and motivation. Students have felt they were taught skills that would be directly useful in any future work field.

It is clear that this program does not compare with a proper training in psychotherapy; however, teaching clinical psychology in Bosnia-Herzegovina today opens the choice between maintaining purely theoretical training or providing at least an introduction to practical clinical work. At this point in time no formal training in psychotherapy is available in the country. Feedback from recently graduated students who participated in this course and who have found a work position is that this course is proving extremely helpful and that their (basic) skills are being appreciated by superiors and colleagues.

One larger project, that includes in addition to the Universities of Sarajevo and Banja Luka four universities of former Yugoslavia (Belgrade, Zagreb, Rijeka, and Pristina), should be mentioned because it has opened some interchange between these universities in the form of collaborative research (including the first project described in the next section) and exchanges of materials like books, tests, and video teaching materials. The most visible outcome of the CLIPSEE (Clinical Psychology at South-East European Universities—Capacity Building) network so far has been the publication of a clinical psychology textbook in the Bosnian, Croatian, and Serbian languages.[4] All but the Munich participants in this work had to overcome both psychological difficulties and major reservations at their respective universities to pursue this piece of collaborative work.

Research projects

In addition to establishing teaching and a curriculum for clinical psychology it was our explicit aim to support the staff and in particular the young assistants in taking up scientific research. Research had not been part of the academic life of the members of the department. The staff of the psychology department had produced very few publications, and those had been books in the Bosnian language. They had no publications in international journals. A great deal of motivational work was necessary to kindle an interest. Seminars in methodology were offered by Steve Powell, project manager of CLIPSEE. Methodological supervision for research projects was regularly provided by members of the Munich faculty and visiting professors from Croatia. By 2003, almost the entire staff was now involved in research either for a doctoral degree or in collaboration with Munich colleagues.[5]

Research projects were conducted with populations of children, adolescents, and adults (mostly traumatized mothers). Examples of our research with children and adolescents are presented in the following sections.

Translation and adaptation of the Achenbach (ASEBA) battery for children and adolescents into Bosnian, Croatian, Serbian, and Albanian

One important preliminary to our research projects was the adaptation to Bosnian of an assessment measure. Thus support for research was geared toward providing researchers with an established and internationally used diagnostic instrument as well as furthering their knowledge about trauma psychology.

As a first step we translated and adapted the Achenbach battery for children and adolescents into Bosnian, and as a second step we investigated a group of schoolchildren from Sarajevo and Gracanica (a small town sixty kilometers from Sarajevo) using the Bosnian version of the YSR (Youth Self-Report), CBCL 4-18 (Children's Behavior Checklist for Parents), and TRF (Teacher's Report Form). The results of this study of Bosnian schoolchildren aged seven to seventeen years and conducted in 2000 (five years after the war) have been presented at conferences.[6] Papers describing the factorial structure of these instruments, the distribution of the symptoms and problems in the Bosnian sample, and covariations of problems with traumatic stress are in preparation.

Effects of separation from or death of father

Possible research topics in postwar Bosnia-Herzegovina were shockingly plentiful. One topic that was frequently brought forward by counseling workers and schoolteachers was the effect of losing the father because he died as a soldier or because he was missing and his destiny unknown or because the children had been separated for as long as five years from him. The effects of different kinds of loss on children's psychological well-being and development are the focus of a research project carried out by Zvizdic and Butollo.[7] For their study a sample of 816 younger adolescents, aged ten to fifteen years and living in Sarajevo, were contacted in 1997 and 1998. A number of these adolescents had suffered traumatic loss (25 percent, death or killing of father, 25 percent, disappearance of father, presumably dead; 25 percent, separation from father during the war; 25 percent, never separated from father). The four groups of respondents differed significantly in their levels of posttraumatic adjustment. Disappearance of the father seems to have the most devastating effect, especially on boys.[8]

A consecutive study was conducted with forty women, whose husbands were missing. Under group conditions (four groups of ten women each), "talking about" the missing husband was compared to "talking to" the missing husband, in dialogue work using the Gestalt therapy empty chair method. Participants in the latter condition benefited more from the intervention; however, the women who had participated in the groups using "talking about" the husband also showed improvement on depression scales and general adjustment scales. The children of the women who participated in this study benefited indirectly, as was shown by questionnaire results.[9]

Returnee children:—Wings of Hope (WOH) reintegration program

One other large-scale problem was the fate of returnee children. Those children had spent the war years with relatives abroad or in homes and boarding schools in other countries. Seventy percent of these children had spent the war years in Germany, and 30 percent had been in other European countries, mostly Austria and Sweden. Because we had considerable experience of cooperating with refugee organizations in Munich, we were very interested in the fate of these children after their return.

Readaptation into the school system. Refugee children, though a highly disturbed group, have so far not attracted a great deal of research interest on their return to their home countries.

The main aim of the program applied to the refugee children in Bosnia, and funded by Wings of Hope, was to support the reintegration of returnee children into the changed Bosnian society, helping them to enhance their knowledge of the Bosnian language, to adapt to the Bosnian school system, and to integrate into their peer groups. Over 1,300 children and adolescents in Bosnia participated in the program. Saturday classes were organized by teachers, who had been trained by E. Cehic, a professor at Sarajevo University, in the following areas: information about the problems and difficulties the returnee children had to face, exchange of information about the time the children had spent in Germany, activities that improve the social climate in the classroom and activities to improve the children's resources (sports, arts). If necessary, children received language classes in Bosnian. Courses were also offered for those children who were interested in maintaining their knowledge of the German language. One specific problem was the relationship between the returnees and the nondisplaced children. The children, particularly the older ones, who had spent the war years at home tended to look down on the returnee children, who had escaped from the war.

The differential effects of the WOH reintegration program have been examined. In summary, the results of our analyses indicate that younger children and girls seem to improve more than older pupils and boys in their knowledge of the Bosnian and German languages and also to do better with school integration.

According to the teacher's perception of the overall improvement of the children, younger children who participated continuously in the program and had emotional problems had the highest gains.[10]

Social and emotional components of the reintegration process. The aim of a qualitative study by M. Bruer, M. Gavranidou, S. Powell, E. Cehic, and W. Butollo was to learn more about the social and emotional situations of the returnee children. These researchers analyzed the essays of 115 returnee children, aged ten to seventeen years, in one school in Sarajevo. As hypothesized, these children reported numerous reintegration difficulties and problems such as adjustment problems in relation to the now new society, social isolation, feelings of sadness, and language and other school problems. Loneliness and isolation emerged as the strongest emotional problems for both girls and boys. There were, however, a number of gender-specific emotional reactions. Boys reported more often than girls that they had problems in all school subjects, and they seemed to have more severe problems with readaptation to the new-old home country. When boys talked about support, it had come through peers, whereas girls felt they were receiving help from teachers and family. The emotions described by girls were more often grief and sadness, whereas the boys talked about shame, boredom, and anger. These results stress the importance of gender-specific interventions and therapeutic programs.[11]

Coping with trauma

A longitudinal research project conducted by Durakovic-Belko was the only project already under way when our collaboration with the University of Sarajevo began. It deals with the interplay of disposition, traumatic stress, and developmental outcome. The study is designed to examine the extent to which dispositional characteristics, particular aspects of traumatic events and of the posttraumatic environment, and cognitive assessments and ways of coping determine the quality of adolescents' adjustment to war traumas. A sample of 393 adolescents, with an average age of seventeen years, was involved in the study. The major parameters, investigated by means of questionnaires, were cognitive appraisal personality and sociodemographic variables.

The results showed that traumatic experiences due to uncontrollable events were judged as uncontrollable in nearly 100 percent of the cases. Only a very few subjects saw these experiences also as a challenge, an attitude that could be interpreted as protective adaptation.

It was a matter of concern that evaluation of war events as irreconcilable loss was very high. Taking the experience of uncontrollability and helplessness into account, it is not surprising, that wishful thinking, daydreaming, and a fatalistic attitude were the most frequently chosen *coping mechanisms*. In contrast to the results of other investigations, expression of emotions and social support were rarely used as coping strategies. In accordance with previous research, personality characteristics were a better predictor than environmental factors for the individual choice of coping mechanism.[12]

Further directions

From our own research projects and from studies presented at *The Symposium on Psychosocial Consequences of War*, held by the faculty of philosophy at Sarajevo University,[13] and the work in the CLIPSEE cooperation project, we draw our suggestions for the future:

First, the studies conducted in Bosnia and other areas of the former Yugoslavia show that the war had devastating effects on children and adolescents, with PTSD and depression as the most prevalent psychopathological consequences. Also, the studies demonstrate the necessity of intervention. Therapeutic support as soon as possible in whatever form (specific treatment of PTSD, nonspecific treatments for mental stabilization, and supportive training and interventions for parents and caregivers) for children and adolescents who have experienced war can not only lead to healing and positive development but also be conducive to peace.

Second, the long-term impact of war in the former Yugoslavia should be examined. An interest here is not only the prevalence of PTSD in follow-up studies but also the examination of personality changes and developmental aspects (individual's ability to fulfill developmental tasks like mating, dating, work, parenting, and so forth). Furthermore, because of the many intervention programs that took place in this area during and after the war, interesting information may be gathered about the differential effects of specific and nonspecific treatment for children and youth in war and postwar societies.

Third, a political implication of the studies conducted in the former Yugoslavia concerns taking children out of war zones. The results stress the necessity of the immediate evacuation of children to safer and war-free places. In comparisons between children who were taken to destinations farther away from the war, like Germany, Austria, and Sweden, and children who were taken to Croatia, the former group was less severely disturbed than the latter. With funding of our work in Bosnia-Herzegovina coming to an end, it is our hope that the work we were able to conduct has set sound foundations for the continuation of successful teaching and research in the region, including continuing cooperation among the universities of the CLIPSEE program. Many personal contacts have been made between staff members and among students of these six universities through a student exchange program. Ongoing research is likely to maintain the link between these universities, and it may be strengthened further by future research projects.

Notes

1. Garton Ash, T. (1999). *History of the present.* Harmondsworth, England: Penguin.

2. Butollo, W. (1996). Psychotherapy integration for war traumatization: A training project in central Bosnia. *European Psychologist, 1*(2), 140–146.

3. Butollo, W., Röper, G., Gavranidou, M., & Maurer, T. (1995). *Basic skills in psychotherapy: Teaching manual for internal use.* Munich: Institute of Psychology.

4. Biro, M., & Butollo, W. (2003). *Clinical psychology.* Novi Sad, Serbia, and Montenegro: W. Futura Publications.

5. Powell, S. (2003). *Quality of life after the war.* (Final report to the Volkswagen Foundation.)

6. See, for example, Gavranidou, M. (2001, March 27–31). *Gender specific adaptations to trauma.* Paper presented at the First World Congress on Women's Mental Health, Berlin; Gavranidou, M., Powell, S., Tvrtkovic, J., & Pasic, E. (2002, February 23–27). *Psychological problems of children and adolescents in post-war Bosnia.* Paper presented at the Fourteenth Congress of Klinische Psychologie Psychotherapie und Beratung, Berlin.

7. Zvizdic, S., & Butollo, W. (2000, July 7–8). *Posttraumatic adjustment of younger adolescents who suffered loss or separation from their fathers.* Paper presented at *The Symposium on Psychosocial Consequences of War,* Sarajevo, Bosnia-Herzegovina.

8. Zvizdic, S., & Butollo, W. (2001). War-related loss of father and persistent depressive reactions in early adolescents. *European Psychologist, 6*(3), 204–214.

9. Butollo, W., Zvizdic, S., & Powell, S. (In preparation). *Dialogical exposure in the treatment of trauma and loss.*

10. Gavranidou, M., Cehic, E., Powell, S., & Pasic, E. (2003). Differential effects of a non-specific school-program on returnee children. In S. Powell &

E. Durakovic-Belko (Eds.), *The psychosocial consequences of war* (pp. 251–254). Sarajevo, Bosnia-Herzegovina: UNICEF.

11. Bruer, M., Gavranidou, M., Powell, S., Cehic, E., & Butollo, W. (In press). Returnee children in Bosnia: Conflicts, coping, problems. *Psychotherapie in Psychiatrie, Klinische Psychologie.*

12. Durakovic-Belko, E. (2000, July 7–8). *Facing traumatic stress: Role of some personality characteristics, socio-demographic characteristics, environment factors and cognitive assessments.* Paper presented at The Symposium on Psychosocial Consequences of War, Sarajevo, Bosnia-Herzegovina.

13. Gavranidou, M. (2003). Overview of results regarding children and young people. In S. Powell & E. Durakovic-Belko (Eds.), *The psychosocial consequences of war* (pp. 127–136). Sarajevo, Bosnia-Herzegovina: UNICEF.

GISELA RÖPER *is senior lecturer at the University of Munich and guest professor at the University of Sarajevo.*

MARIA GAVRANIDOU *is professor at the Institute for Psychology, Department of Public Health, Munich.*

Given the magnitude of the possible exposure and duration of distress evidenced by Iraqi children, there is strong reason to expect that this, in combination with malnutrition and reduced school attendance, will dramatically reduce their learning potential.

6

Threat in the life of Iraqi children

Atle Dyregrov, Magne Raundalen

FOLLOWING THE 1991 Gulf War we were part of what was called The International Study Team, documenting the effects of the war and the United Nations sanctions on the Iraqi civilian population. In a study following a group of ninety-three children in Baghdad over the two years after the war, we found that children continued to experience sadness and remained afraid of losing their families. Trauma scores continued to be high, indicating that symptoms persisted, with somewhat diminished intensity over time. It was concluded that the psychological impact of war on children is not over when the fighting ceases.[1]

For the past year, and increasingly over the last months before the outbreak of war in Iraq, the threat was very high in Iraq. There is some indication that threat to survival is especially important for the development of posttraumatic symptoms in both adults[2] and children.[3] In a study we carried out following the massacres in Rwanda in 1994,[4] threat to one's life was the factor that evidenced the strongest influence on two debilitating traumatic stress reactions,

NEW DIRECTIONS FOR YOUTH DEVELOPMENT, NO. 98, SUMMER 2003 © WILEY PERIODICALS, INC.

intrusion of negative sensory memories and avoidance of any experience that might remind the child of the threat.

In January 2003, some members of the original International Study Team, supplemented by other experts, carried out a new mission to Iraq to look at the consequences of a new war on Iraqi children. We were responsible for the child mental well-being part of this mission.

Effects of the threat of war on Iraq children

Iraqi families have lived with sanctions and the results of massive bombing for more than ten years. This has led to poverty, malnutrition, and death; economic depression; and problems with sanitation, electricity, and water. Regarding young Iraqi children, a UNICEF report states:

Exhausted parents who can hardly meet the family's basic needs are naturally less sensitive and caring towards their children, and deprived children often add through their consequent difficult behaviour to parents' distress. Families whose resources for loving care are depleted through long-term multiple stressors can no longer provide their children with a sense of belonging, which is necessary to promote young children's curiosity, exploratory activities and tolerance for unfamiliar situations. Finally, the home environment of many young children has become depleted of essential commodities, toys, books and other opportunities for self-directed learning and achievement.[5]

Although not as high a level of threat as in 2002 and 2003, the threat of a war has been constant in the lives of the Iraqi children over the last eight years. Many children do not know any other reality; they have lived with this threat all their life. Clinically, we know that living with uncertainty takes its toll. Over time it depletes energy, with tiredness and exhaustion often more acutely felt when the danger is over. Little is known about the ways children experience the threat of a possible war. To our knowledge no one has ever studied this. Will children adapt "naturally" and therefore give little thought to the threat? Will they seek out information to try to cope, or will they try to reduce their exposure to news and information to maintain as normal a situation as possible?

These were some of the questions we wanted to learn more about by talking to children directly.[6]

What did we do?

In the fourth week of January 2003 we visited twenty-one families and had in-depth interviews with eighty-five children and youngsters from the ages of four to eighteen years. The families were recruited from different areas of Baghdad and Basra by door-to-door knocking, without any previous appointment. In addition, we visited two schools and collected 232 questionnaires from school-children aged ten to sixteen years (M = 12.7). The three-page questionnaire consisted of the Iraqi Child & Adolescent Questionnaire, the Impact of the Threat Questionnaire, and the Birleson Depression Inventory, all soliciting information about the mental consequences resulting from the children's present situation.

Visiting families

Our interviews of the children were constructed to get an in-depth impression of how children in different age groups experienced the war threat. We had access to the families without any government interference and were able to go from door to door in different neighborhoods. All the families welcomed us and cooperated in a very friendly and open manner. Parents understood and respected our wish to talk to children alone when we explained that it was our experience that children were more open and talkative without the parents present. For some families we did not find this appropriate, for example, when we needed parental cooperation to talk to the smallest children. After the interview we all gathered together, and we reiterated the aim of the study and reported on our interaction with the children. The interview was semistructured. In place of prewritten questions it identified specific issues to be covered. One issue was how the present situation and the threat of an armed attack affected the children's daily lives, including their psychological reactions, with special attention to fear, sadness, and anger. A second issue was communication about their thoughts and worries both at home and at school. Whom could the child talk to for updated information, explanation, and comfort?

Alone with the fear

With few exceptions the children reported that the imminent threat of war was influencing their daily lives. They thought about the threat every day and were very fearful about what could happen. At the same time there had been little communication with parents, teachers, or friends about the emotional aspects of the threat. Parents obviously had not found a good way to inform or comfort their children, and the children were not confronting the parents with penetrating questions. Children's fear had a life of its own, seldom touched by communicating with others. They listened to news and watched TV but were often confused by what was reported or said. Watching the news increased their fear, but at the same time it was difficult not to listen to the news, either because they wanted to know what had happened or because rooming conditions made it impossible to refrain from listening and viewing. Yet some youth were very clear about not watching news: "I run away as soon as the news starts."

We understand that parents struggle with this and that their avoidance of communicating about threat and fear with their children is normal. It is not easy to transform one's own fear and worry for the future into calming and comforting language to children.

Even children as young as four and five had concepts of real physical threat from bombs and guns—destroying of houses, burning homes, and killing of people—and thought that in the end, referring to their own families, "we will all die." The youngest children had some mental protection owing to their lack of understanding: one girl thought that she was protected when her sister put the blanket over her head, and another was comforted by the mere fact that her brother had a knife in his room. Parents were surprised to hear how much their preschoolers feared the situation (for these youngest children we had a parent present during our interviews).

The fear most children felt concerned the death of family members and their fear for their own lives. In addition to their fear, the general life situation of the children often resulted in a state of fatigue, resignation, and sadness. They could discuss the prospect for peace and express hope for peace and even optimism for the future, but in the end they were often resigned and stated, "There will be a war." They spoke about having adapted to the situation, but this adaptation had a resigned and depressive quality to it.

Questionnaire data

The responses to the questionnaire showed that almost all children were concerned about a possible war; they worried that they might not live to become adults and that something bad would happen to them or someone in their family. The high numbers of children that reported many or very many headaches (61 percent) reflected physical consequences of this constant threat and tension. More than 70 percent feared very much that something would happen to their family. Despite this they were optimistic and had hopes that things would improve for them, and they enjoyed playing and fun activities.

Questionnaire data showed a high level of intrusive thinking about the threat. Although they did not want to think about it, the thoughts often came. This may partly explain that 35 percent often had attention and concentration difficulties (another 25 percent had this sometimes), but malnourishment and difficult living conditions may sustain or increase these problems. The threat often led to waves of strong feelings, including alertness and watchfulness when it was not necessary. When we used the Impact of Event Scale for children[7] as many as 78.8 percent scored above the recommended cutoff point of 17. However, our use of this scale was a bit unorthodox, as the children were asked when filling in the thirteen items to think not of a specific event but about the threat of war.

The Birleson Depression Inventory also reflected a group on which the situation was taking its toll. The recommended cutoff score is 17, and 70.7 percent of the Iraqi children scored above this level. Again there should be some caution when interpreting these results, as the score may be inflated by lack of food and malnourishment (items on the inventory include "I get stomach aches" and "I enjoy my food"). But even after we took this possibility into account, the group was depressed, whether as a result of the economic sanctions or of the threat of war. Almost 40 percent of the children reported that they felt life was not worth living most of the time, and an additional 17 percent sometimes felt that way. Nearly half of them felt very lonely most of the time. About one-quarter of them never slept well, and a similar number sometimes slept well. Many suffered from bad dreams that further jeopardized their sleep.

Conclusion

Given the duration of distress evidenced by Iraqi children before the war, and the exposure to a variety of war stressors during the war, there is strong reason to expect that this, in combination with unforeseeable consequences of malnutrition and reduced school attendance can dramatically reduce the learning potential of youth, especially among the poor. The mental resources of Iraqi parents have been depleted over a long period of time, and in combination with other negative health effects this may have a catastrophic effect on children's mental health.

With the history of sanctions, the long-standing threat, and the exposure to war stressors, rapid access to nutritious food, clean water and electricity, and improved security will be important to restore children's physical well-being. This, together with a rapid return to normal schooling, will also be a good remedial for lessening children's fear. However, with the large number of children exposed to traumatic stressors such as bombing, shelling, and loss of loved ones, our findings from the last Gulf war and from before the recent war started imply that many children will suffer from sadness anxiety and posttraumatic reactions. There is an imminent need for the government, UNICEF, and other NGOs to instigate programs that may contain and mitigate the situation. Information must be provided for parents on how they can communicate with and help their children in relation to the war. Unfortunately, many children are left with their own fear and fantasies, with little adult communication or understanding. In addition to advising parents about the need for talking more directly with their children about how they feel, parents can be made more conscious about the effect of news on children, and about how overhearing adults talk about the news strongly affects the child. Open communication, where children can express their thoughts (and fantasies) to listening adults, can in itself alleviate some reactions, but this will require adults who can be calm, reflective, and listening.

Programs need to be put in place by the government, UNICEF, and NGOs to assist children in kindergartens and schools that take into account how the long period of threat is a contributing influence on reactions to the war. With a child population already run down by years of sanctions and threat, the challenges for good psychosocial interventions in the wake of the war are formidable. Unfortunately, little is known about the interplay between prewar mental exhaustion and exposure to trauma during war. Although all children can receive normalizing information and help to continue normal development through outreach school programs, more seriously traumatized children can be screened in order to enter groups where they can learn strategies helpful in reducing posttraumatic distress. One such model that has shown great promise is the manual developed under the auspices of the Children and War Foundation.[8]

Notes

1. Dyregrov, A., Gjestad, R., & Raundalen, M. (2002). Children exposed to warfare: A longitudinal study. *Journal of Traumatic Stress, 15,* 59–68.

2. Fontana, A., Rosenheck, R., & Brett, E. (1992). War zone traumas and posttraumatic stress disorder symptomatology. *Journal of Nervous and Mental Disease, 180,* 748–755; Hauff, E., & Vaglum, P. (1993). Vietnamese boat refugees: The influence of war and flight traumatization on mental health on arrival in the country of resettlement. *Acta Psychiatrica Scandinavica, 88,* 162–168.

3. Carlson, E. B., & Rosser-Hogan, R. (1994). Cross-cultural response to trauma: A study of traumatic experiences and posttraumatic symptoms in Cambodian refugees. *Journal of Traumatic Stress, 7,* 43–58.

4. Dyregrov, A., Gupta, L., Gjestad, R., & Mukanoheli, E. (2000). Trauma exposure and psychological reactions to genocide among Rwandan children. *Journal of Traumatic Stress, 13,* 3–21.

5. UNICEF and Iraq Ministry of Health. (1999, July). *Child and Maternal Mortality Survey 1999* (Preliminary Report). New York: UNICEF.

6. The entire report on the consequences of a possible war on children is available on-line at http://www.warchild.ca/report.asp

7. Smith, P., Perrin, S., Dyregrov, A., & Yule, W. (2003). Principal components analysis of the Impact of Event Scale with children in war. *Personality and Individual Differences, 34,* 315–322.

8. Smith, P., Dyregrov, A., & Yule, W. (1998). *Children and war: Teaching recovery techniques.* Bergen: Children and War Foundation.

ATLE DYREGROV *is a clinical and research psychologist and is the founding director of the Center for Crisis Psychology in Bergen, Norway.*

MAGNE RAUNDALEN *is a child psychologist who has over twenty years experience working with children affected by war. Former president of UNICEF Norway, he now heads a national program for traumatized refugees in Norway.*

Response to the events of 9/11 evidenced the need for greater local and national capacity to meet the needs of children and families before, during, and after future attacks

7

Time frames

William W. Harris

WE ARE ALL SCARED. The Maryland snipers, the Orange alert, conflicting advice and instructions about the use of duct tape and plastic sheeting in the event of a chemical or biological attack, a war with Iraq, a possible confrontation with North Korea—how are we supposed to process this information? How are we supposed to deal with our own fear, much less the fears of our children?

As the saying goes, "The trouble with the future is that it's not what it used to be." Indeed, an American's view of the present and the future is completely different today from what it was prior to September 11, 2001.

I approach these questions and issues from the point of view of a long-time lobbyist for children who is interested in the provision of optimal developmental opportunities so that children can attain their optimal levels of success. I consider three different time frames: before 9/11, the period surrounding 9/11, and the future.

NEW DIRECTIONS FOR YOUTH DEVELOPMENT, NO. 98, SUMMER 2003 © WILEY PERIODICALS, INC.

Pre-9/11

In September of 2000, I wrote an Op-Ed piece about our country's consideration—or lack thereof—of preparing children for school.[1] Almost a decade prior to this, Governor Bill Clinton (then head of the National Governors' Association) had gone to President George H. Bush, and together they had established a bipartisan set of education goals for the year 2000. The first goal was that by the year 2000, all children would arrive in school ready to learn. In the Op-Ed, I wrote that "the plans and resources required to implement (this goal) have neither been identified nor committed," and that it was "time for each presidential candidate to be clear about how his administration would address school readiness. Each [should] provide specific plans and commitments for implementing and paying for a school readiness program so that the public will support this priority." I concluded by saying that if there were no presidential or Congressional mandate to prepare children to arrive at school ready to learn, "the country will continue to wage only skirmishes for young children, even as most of us know that to address the school readiness issue successfully, we must declare and wage a protracted war." Little did I know at the time, that the notion of protracted war would become part of the parlance and everyday environment of Americans post-9/11.

Prior to 9/11, the politics around poor children, those children who are more often at risk, who often live in more chronically traumatic environments, who are more likely to arrive at school not ready to learn, and who suffer from a lack of services and from a national lack of commitment to provide for their well-being were not doing well.

Approximately one in four U.S. children was in poverty before 9/11, approximately the same fraction as we find today. Whether this number will move up in the next months and years as a result of the economic downturn and state and federal budget cuts is unclear. It is clear that our country's commitment to these poor children's preparation for school remains inexplicably deficient.

As we prepare for this year's reauthorization of the Head Start Act, fewer than 4 percent of eligible children are being served by the premier program for school readiness—Early Head Start.

Despite the success the program has attained and despite the research that shows that it works, the commitment and evidence to expand it to more eligible children does not appear in the administration's budget for 2004.

Who are these eligible children? They are disproportionately children of color who live in conditions of chronic risk and traumatic situations. They are the same children who appear in the various epidemiological studies in the trauma literature, but they are often referred to as if they came from separate populations. These are the children who have been abused and neglected, who have witnessed domestic violence, who inhabit the juvenile justice system, who abuse substances, who drop out of school and fail in school. These are the children who become pregnant when they are teenagers and often have been sexually abused or raped before they became pregnant with their first child. I continue to be astounded that we refer to these children in these different situations as if they were different children, when in fact, sadly, too often they are the same children.

How has our country dealt with these children historically? We have devised, in one congressional committee, programs to deliver on the ground in various communities services that address the "health needs" of children; in another committee, services for the "education needs" of the child; and in yet another committee, services for "trauma exposure treatment needs." It is as if the U.S. Congress were structured to address children's problems as though children came in separate parts and were not whole people. The analogy would be an emergency room that sets the broken arm and the broken leg of a child injured in a severe accident but provides no services for the child's concussion and internal injuries.

This piecemeal approach to programs does not serve our children well. Some data suggest that up to one-sixth of Head Start children come to the program with a background of untreated trauma-related experiences, that children with disabilities have at least twice the likelihood of other children of having an untreated trauma-related experience, and that an overwhelming majority of children in juvenile justice, substance abuse, teenage pregnancy, and similar programs have had serious trauma-related experiences.

Yet we do little to assess, diagnose, and treat these same children even as we understand that not doing so will most likely have an adverse impact on their school readiness and their educational progress and can have a definite negative impact on their social skills, emotional well-being, and healthy developmental trajectory. A cynic might describe the situation this way. If we do not assess or diagnose these children, we do not have to say that there is a problem. If we say there is no problem, we do not have to identify and treat it. And if we do not identify and treat it, we do not have to pay for it.

Prior to 9/11, the Congress and the administration usually provided programs for children and families in parts and pieces rather than in the ecological context that child development people understand to be the appropriate approach—dealing with the whole child in the context of the family, the community, and the culture.

9/11

Then came 9/11. There was a declaration of war by the United States government on terrorism throughout the world. And how did America proceed to address the mental health issues of the impact of 9/11 on America's children?

Marshall McLuhan, the sage Canadian media analyst, once observed that Americans went forward by looking in the rearview mirror. Looking at the world after 9/11 in the old ways was clearly not the way the administration said it wanted to move ahead. The head of the Joint Chiefs of Staff, Richard B. Myers, put it this way: "You know, if you try to quantify what we're doing today in terms of previous conventional wars, you're making a huge mistake," he said. "That is 'old think' and that will not help you analyze what we're doing. And that's what we've been trying to tell you for three days. It's a different kind of conflict."[2]

It is a different kind of war requiring a different approach. But a "new approach to war" was not in evidence on 9/11 in New York City. As many good people scrambled into New York to offer and provide services for the hundreds of thousands of traumatized children, youth, and families, the lack of a unified communications strategy and structure was immediately apparent. Indeed, a total lack of preparedness was evidenced throughout most systems.

Our government's response of establishing a brand-new super-agency of "homeland security" is an interesting abstraction, but if the fire chief can't talk to the police chief in a middle-sized city two years later, how much have we really learned? What have we really accomplished in terms of preparedness?

Even as Israel today is trying to prepare for the next war in the context of continuous suicide bombings and assassinations, it is perfectly clear that coordination across fields of medicine, response services, military and police services, and the like is extraordinarily complex to understand, install, and manage. Our nation has critical work ahead of it to prepare for a future attack.

The future

A study conducted by the New York City Department of Education after 9/11, interviewing over 8,000 school-age children from fourth to twelfth grade, discovered that a full 64 percent of the children had experienced significant trauma *prior* to 9/11. This suggests that the trauma of 9/11, piled upon the previous unresolved traumas, could present these children with real difficulties in moving ahead with their normal developmental trajectories in school and in their social and personal lives.

Some of us have begun to ask questions about the provision of mental health and psychosocial services for children exposed to trauma. What happens if in the not-too-distant future someone were to drop some chemicals or some "bugs" in a regular-sized city somewhere in America? What would we do? Are we really prepared? What is preparedness? Whose responsibility is it?

The recent creation of the Department of Homeland Security suggests a federal role in organizing federal departments to deploy policies and resources to the state and local levels. But in reality, how will this be achieved?

Decision-making powers will have to be distributed outside of the federal government, presumably to state, county, and locally responsible agencies, so that they can in fact prepare for, provide for, and deliver necessary services and also assess the effectiveness of their preparedness to protect their local child populations.

Given the national focus of the Red Cross, with its state and local agencies; the National Guard and its administrative functioning details; and the many governor's and mayor's offices, how do we begin to go about this awesome task?

One approach would involve state and local entities in preparing a dynamic map of where children are throughout the day, throughout the week, throughout the year. By identifying where children are and in whose care they are, we could place their locations, according to their ages, on a map. This map could then be merged with a map of existing and potential social service delivery assets in the same geographical areas. Looking at these maps together and seeing where social service assets and child populations overlap would reveal who the adults were who would need to be trained to deliver trauma-related services to children. The technology already exists for this kind of program mapping.

Although it is clear that we can identify and train adults, from Head Start teachers to child-care workers to schoolteachers and the clergy, it becomes apparent immediately that children are spending more time outside of school and other formal settings than in those settings. They are at home with their families or elsewhere in the community. This suggests that were an attack to occur at a time outside regular institutional hours, the role of the media in communicating with children, parents, and families and with other adults who care for children would be critical.

Talking to the media about training them on how to work in an emergency is an extremely difficult challenge for a media outsider. Most media professionals believe that they know what is best for their audiences, and they resent or will not tolerate any outside intervention, especially from the government. One answer might be to establish a partnership among first responders, trauma experts, child development experts, and the media—a long-range working partnership. The work of this partnership would be to identify separate and coordinated roles and tasks for each stakeholder and determine the ways all the stakeholders can work together if or when another attack occurs.

Leaders from the media, responder, and trauma care provider communities must come forward immediately to put this partnership together. In the event of subsequent major attacks in America, the degree to which we minimize the pain and anxiety from the attack and maximize the community resilience and the resilience of the children, youth, and families affected by the trauma could be greatly increased by the success of such a partnership.

It is also clear that we do not currently have sufficient capacity to train all Head Start teachers, all child-care teachers, all schoolteachers, all first responders, and so forth, with the skills and strategies needed to address and deal with the psychosocial needs of children who will have been traumatized by an attack. Capacity building must be one of our first orders of business. We will need to have these adults working with children. We must begin to develop the capacity to train more people to train others so that our nation will be ready to better serve the psychosocial needs of our children in the event of another national emergency.

Questions remain: Whose responsibility is it to move forward at the national, state, and local levels with this plan to address these issues, and in what contexts does this responsibility assert itself? Addressing these issues only from the Department of Homeland Security—from the federal top down to the local grassroots—will neither work nor inspire any confidence whatsoever in the general population. How will we develop local and state competence? How will we develop more local capacity?

The images of 9/11 are forever ingrained in each of us and in our children. The question is, How will we move ahead to develop strengths and capacities to address the future for our children? This is our obligation to our children and their future. If not us, who? If not now, when?

Notes

1. Harris, W. H. (Sept. 27, 2000). Invest in children. (Op-ed.) *Miami Herald.*
2. Woodward, R. (2002). *Bush at War.* New York: Simon and Schuster, p. 220.

WILLIAM W. HARRIS *is the head of KidsPac, a political action committee he founded in 1981.*

Index

Notes for Contributors

New Directions for Youth Development: Theory, Practice, and Research is a quarterly publication focusing on current contemporary issues challenging the field of youth development. A defining focus of the journal is the relationship among theory, research, and practice. In particular, *NDYD* is dedicated to recognizing resilience as well as risk, and healthy development of our youth as well as the difficulties of adolescence. The journal is intended as a forum for provocative discussion that reaches across the worlds of academia, service, philanthropy, and policy.

In the tradition of the New Directions series, each volume of the journal addresses a single, timely topic, although special issues covering a variety of topics are occasionally commissioned. We welcome submissions of both volume topics and individual articles. All articles should specifically address the implications of theory for practice and research directions, and how these arenas can better inform one another. Articles may focus on any aspect of youth development; all theoretical and methodological orientations are welcome.

If you would like to be an *issue editor*, please submit an outline of no more than four pages (single spaced, 12 point type) that includes a brief description of your proposed topic and its significance along with a brief synopsis of individual articles (including tentative authors and a working title for each chapter).

If you would like to be an *author*, please submit first a draft of an abstract of no more than 1,500 words, including a two-sentence synopsis of the article; send this to the managing editor.

For all prospective issue editors or authors:

- Please make sure to keep accessibility in mind, by illustrating theoretical ideas with specific examples and explaining technical terms in nontechnical language. A busy practitioner who may not have an extensive research background should be well served by our work.

- Please keep in mind that references should be limited to twenty-five to thirty. Authors should make use of case examples to illustrate their ideas, rather than citing exhaustive research references. You may want to recommend two or three key articles, books, or Websites that are influential in the field, to be featured on a resource page. This can be used by readers who want to delve more deeply into a particular topic.
- All reference information should be listed as endnotes, rather than including author names in the body of the article or footnotes at the bottom of the page.

Back Issue/Subscription Order Form

Copy or detach and send to:

Jossey-Bass, A Wiley Company, 989 Market Street, San Francisco CA 94103-1741

Call or fax toll-free: Phone 888-378-2537; Fax 888-481-2665

Back Issues: Please send me the following issues at $28 each
(Important: please include issue ISBN)

_____

_____

$ _____   Total for single issues

$ _____   SHIPPING CHARGES: SURFACE   Domestic Canadian
                              First Item $5.00 $6.00
                              Each Add'l Item $3.00 $1.50
              Please call for next day, second day, or international shipping rates.

Subscriptions   Please ❑ start ❑ renew my subscription to *New Directions for Youth Development* at the following rate:

U.S.	❑ Individual $75	❑ Institutional $149
Canada	❑ Individual $75	❑ Institutional $189
All Others	❑ Individual $99	❑ Institutional $223
Online Subscription		❑ Institutional $149

**For more information about online subscriptions visit
www.interscience.wiley.com**

− _____   Are you eligible for our **Student Subscription Rate**? Attach a copy of your current Student Identification Card and deduct 20% from the regular subscription rate.

$ _____   Total single issues and subscriptions (Add appropriate sales tax for your state for single issue orders. No sales tax for U.S. subscriptions. Canadian residents, add GST for subscriptions and single issues.)

❑Payment enclosed (U.S. check or money order only)
❑VISA ❑ MC ❑ AmEx # _____ Exp. Date _____
Your credit card payment will be charged to John Wiley & Sons.

Signature _____ Day Phone _____
❑ Bill Me (U.S. institutional orders only. Purchase order required.)

Purchase order # _____
Federal Tax ID13559302   **GST 89102 8052**

Name _____

Address _____

_____

Phone _____ E-mail _____

PROMOTION CODE ND3

Other Titles Available

NEW DIRECTIONS FOR YOUTH DEVELOPMENT: THEORY, PRACTICE, AND RESEARCH
Gil G. Noam, Editor-in-Chief

and about the related concepts of thriving and well-being, as well as current and needed policy strategies, "best practice" in youth-serving programs, and promising community-based efforts to marshal the developmental assets of individuals and communities to enhance thriving among youth.
ISBN 0-7879-6338-0

YD94 **Youth Development and After-School Time: A Tale of Many Cities**
Gil G. Noam, Beth Miller
This issue looks at exciting citywide and cross-city initiatives in after-school time. It presents case studies of youth-related work that combines large-scale policy, developmental thinking, innovative programming, as well as research and evaluation. Chapters discuss efforts of community-based organizations, museums, universities, schools, and clinics who are joining forces, sharing funding and other resources and jointly creating a system of after-school care and education.
ISBN 0-7879-6337-2

YD93 **A Critical View of Youth Mentoring**
Jean E. Rhodes
Mentoring has become an almost essential aspect of youth development and is expanding beyond the traditional one-to-one, volunteer, community-based mentoring. This volume provides evidence of the benefits of enduring high-quality mentoring programs, as well as apprenticeships, advisories, and other relationship-based programs that show considerable promise. Authors examine mentoring in the workplace, teacher-student interaction, and the mentoring potential of student advising programs. They also take a critical look at the importance of youth-adult relationships and how a deeper understanding of these relationships can benefit youth mentoring. This issue raises important questions about relationship-based interventions and generates new perspectives on the role of adults in the lives of youth.
ISBN 0-7879-6294-5

YD92 **Zero Tolerance: Can Suspension and Expulsion Keep Schools Safe?**
Russell J. Skiba, Gil G. Noam
Addressing the problem of school violence and disruption requires thoughtful understanding of the complexity of the personal and systemic factors that increase the probability of violence, and designing interventions based on that understanding. This inaugural issue explores the effectiveness of zero tolerance as a tool for promoting school safety and improving student behavior and offer alternative strategies that work.
ISBN 0-7879-1441-X

NEW DIRECTIONS FOR YOUTH DEVELOPMENT IS NOW AVAILABLE ONLINE AT WILEY INTERSCIENCE

What is Wiley InterScience?

Wiley InterScience is the dynamic online content service from John Wiley & Sons delivering the full text of over 300 leading scientific, technical, medical, and professional journals, plus major reference works, the acclaimed *Current Protocols* laboratory manuals, and even the full text of select Wiley print books online.

What are some special features of Wiley InterScience?

Wiley InterScience Alerts is a service that delivers table of contents via e-mail for any journal available on Wiley InterScience as soon as a new issue is published online.
Early View is Wiley's exclusive service presenting individual articles online as soon as they are ready, even before the release of the compiled print issue. These articles are complete, peer-reviewed, and citable.
CrossRef is the innovative multi-publisher reference linking system enabling readers to move seamlessly from a reference in a journal article to the cited publication, typically located on a different server and published by a different publisher.

How can I access Wiley InterScience?

Visit http://www.interscience.wiley.com

Guest Users can browse Wiley InterScience for unrestricted access to journal Tables of Contents and Article Abstracts, or use the powerful search engine.
Registered Users are provided with a *Personal Home Page* to store and manage customized alerts, searches, and links to favorite journals and articles. Additionally, Registered Users can view free Online Sample Issues and preview selected material from major reference works.
Licensed Customers are entitled to access full-text journal articles in PDF, with select journals also offering full-text HTML.

How do I become an Authorized User?

Authorized Users are individuals authorized by a paying Customer to have access to the journals in Wiley InterScience. For example, a university that subscribes to Wiley journals is considered to be the Customer. Faculty, staff and students authorized by the university to have access to those journals in Wiley InterScience are Authorized Users. Users should contact their Library for information on which Wiley journals they have access to in Wiley InterScience.

ASK YOUR INSTITUTION ABOUT WILEY INTERSCIENCE TODAY!

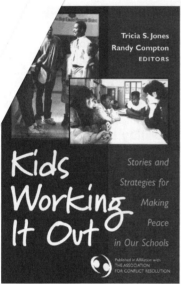